Rave Reviews for Di

Yours is the only show that provides so much useful information jammed into a half hour. Top that off with what should be an award-winning Web site, and you've got a recipe for a hit!

VIVIAN

In comparison to other cooking show hosts, Christine is more professional and well spoken. She knows what she's doing.

STEPHANIE

Your recipes are simple enough for the novice cook and fun enough for any experienced cook.

B. MENOUTIS

You have a great show. You're very informative and straight to the point.

RICHARD

Your Web site is wonderful; it's so user friendly. I like the fact that I can interact with others and get updates on recipes.

KAREN

I really love the way you introduce Asian elements into your cuisine. I often try your recipes, to the delight of my family. Also, my five-year-old daughter mimics your techniques and actually comes up with amazing recipes (not bad for an otherwise picky eater).

Y. WATKINS

Your show has some great tips, wonderful recipes and Christine is an awesome chef!

JOHN

Dish It Out

Simple Recipes That Inspire

Christine Cushing

Prentice
Hall
Canada

A Pearson Company
Toronto

Canadian Cataloguing in Publication Data

Cushing, Christine
    Dish it out: simple recipes that inspire

Includes index.
ISBN 0-13-026815-1

1. Quick and easy cookery. I. Title

TX833.5.C87 2000 641.5'55   C00-930131-3

ISBN 0-13-026815-1

Editorial Director, Trade Division: Andrea Crozier
Acquisitions Editor: Nicole de Montbrun
Copy Editor: Susan Broadhurst
Production Editor: Jodi Lewchuk
Art Direction: Mary Opper
Cover Design and Interior Design: Domenic Macri
Photographs: Per Kristiansen
Author Photo: Bill Milne
Production Manager: Kathrine Pummell
Page Layout: Arlene Edgar

1 2 3 4 5 KR 04 03 02 01 00

Printed and bound in Canada.

Visit the Prentice Hall Canada Web site! Send us your comments,
browse our catalogues, and more. **www.phcanada.com.**

Prentice
Hall
Canada

A Pearson Company

Food is simple

A perfectly red ripe tomato
Drizzled with robust olive oil

Food is inspiration

If only to master
That ethereal homespun phyllo dough

Food is sustenance

A warming bouillabaisse
A steamy, crusty hearth-baked loaf

Food is mystery

A sweet yet peppery taste
Is it ginger, the Asian staple?
Or perhaps allspice, the Caribbean native?

Food is sensual

A satiny, smooth crème brûlée
An earthy, fragrant black truffle risotto

Food is personal

When you know a person's cooking,
You feel better acquainted

Food is ... life

To my parents, who taught me that the only thing better than preparing and savouring a great meal is the anticipation of the next one!

Contents

Acknowledgments

Thanks to my producer Mark Johnston—who came down to the food show, picked me out of the crowd, and made "Dish it Out" a reality—for believing in me and always bringing out the best in me.

To Nicole de Montbrun, my editor at Prentice Hall, for creating a whole new chapter in my life. She made this book possible, believed in me, and allowed me to trust myself and write this book from the heart!

Thanks to David Lehmkuhl, from KitchenAid, for his overwhelming support of this book, and my work. And thanks to John Patrick, for his enthusiastic praise.

To my parents, brother, and family, who have always supported my crazy cooking antics.

To my husband, who encouraged me to leave my full-time restaurant job and follow my heart.

To Life Network, for supporting the show and the book, especially Karen Gelbart, who has been a constant source of encouragement and inspiration.

To Jim Kemp, at Give It a Stir, for always believing I had a great future—and Melissa, for being my biggest fan.

Thanks to everyone at ExtendMedia, for their encouragement and efforts on our site. Special thanks to Julian Wharton, Thomas Wallner, and Patrick Crowe.

Thanks to Domenic Macri, for his vision and beautiful design of the book; Per Kristiansen, for his simple yet inspiring photography; and all the people at Prentice Hall, without whom this book would not be possible.

And to all the friends and chefs that I have worked with over the years, for whom I am truly grateful, especially those at Scaramouche, King Ranch, Presidential Gourmet, and *The Globe and Mail*.

Introduction

Generally, I'm not one to believe in kismet, or fate, but every now and then something happens that I know—undeniably—was meant to be. Such was the case on a spring afternoon when I was busy working at a booth for KitchenAid. It was the Good Food Festival in Toronto and I was pulsing, whipping, and blending my way through the small appliances, answering questions from onlookers huddled around my orange cranberry loaf in progress.

I was fitted with a headset microphone so the audience could hear my every word. At one point during the demo, I found myself gazing at someone who looked vaguely familiar. Without hesitation, or any thought to the microphone, I asked who she was. When she gave her name, I instantly realized she was my grade nine home-economics teacher. Imagine it: Here I was doing a cooking demo for one of my very first cooking instructors! I laughed uproariously at the wonderful irony, oblivious to the fact that the entire audience, and many others at the festival, were in on my little "awakening."

As my laughter subsided, a man approached the stage and handed me a business card that read "Mark Johnston—Executive Producer." Mark said he was looking for the host of a new cooking show. "Would you like to audition?" he asked. I very nearly shouted, "WHAT! ARE YOU KIDDING?" With extreme difficulty, I managed to keep my cool and responded in a very calm voice: "I'm working this booth all weekend, but I should be able to come up with something by Monday morning."

Looking back on that day, my producer and I kill ourselves laughing because, in trying not to seem over-enthusiastic, I came across as Miss I'll-see-if-I-can-squeeze-you-in. Luckily, Mark gave me the benefit of the doubt and said he would courier me the details. After he left, I began to ponder the upcoming audition. What the heck was I going to cook in five minutes? Minute rice was not an option.

I felt for the poor guys who had to work with me the rest of the weekend at the show. Jim, owner of the cookware shop Give It a Stir, had to listen to me yap incessantly about the audition. He kept saying, "They'll pick you for sure."

"Yeah? But I don't even know what to prepare!"

I did, however, remember something Mark had said to me: "Don't worry about what you're going to make; worry about what you're going to say." Keeping that in mind, I decided on a very simple but interesting variation on pizza.

The Monday of the audition, I arrived at the studio wearing jeans and a T-shirt—I wanted to be comfortable so that the producers would focus on the food and what I had to say, not on what I was wearing. As I sat waiting in the green room with a few other candidates, I managed to finally read the audition notes' fine print. "NO JEANS" immediately jumped out at me. That would have been a good thing to notice before getting dressed! I began to get nervous. To make matters worse, the other two women who were auditioning were elegantly attired in suits. By this point I was thinking, "It's all over but the cryin'."

"Christine Cushing," a voice yelled out, "you're up." I scurried to the set, knife bag and food props in hand. The crew was incredibly friendly and helped to pump me up. As I set up and took my mark, they directed me to look at the camera and express, in one minute, why I should get this job. "Are you nervous?" the floor director asked. "No," I said. "All right then, in three, two, one…" Once that little red light went on, I was off to the races. (You never really know how you're going to respond until after the light goes on.) The synopsis of my on-camera plea was that I had a great passion for food, had been cooking most of my life, and loved to tell silly little stories, which I thought made me a good candidate.

As fate would have it, I got the job! And that led to a book contract (by the way, the recipe for the "audition pizza" on page 163).

If you still don't believe that fate had any hand in my "Dishing" It Out, you'll want to know that the day my producer picked me out of the crowd was my birthday. That, and the audition, is now one of my mother's favourite stories. Another favourite story is the one about how she always knew I was going to be a chef because I asked for a plastic oven when I was two. (I am growing a little tired of that "when she was two" bit.) But ultimately, Mom was right—she always is.

It's All Greek to Me!

Al dente: Cooking pasta until it is tender but still has a bite to it. The literal translation from Italian is "to the tooth." Believe me, it's the only way to cook pasta!

Arborio rice: A short-grain Italian rice that is high in starch and used to make risotto. Perfectionists should try superfino arborio or even carneroli—superior grades of rice that yield the creamiest risotto.

Au gratin: A French phrase that refers to a dish prepared with cheese and/or breadcrumbs sprinkled over it and finished under the broiler for a crisp topping. "Gratin" is the noun and "au gratin" describes the style of preparation.

Bain-marie: A water bath used in French culinary terms as a double boiler. Place hot water in a pot and top with a stainless steel bowl. The water should not touch the bottom of the bowl. This ensures even, gentle cooking of custards, sauces, etc. It can also refer to a pan with water used to bake custards like crème brûlée in the oven.

Baton: A French culinary term meaning "shaped like a stick," usually referring to a way of cutting vegetables. I call for batons of beets and apples in the pork stir-fry recipe on page 130.

Bean threads: Unusual Asian noodles made from dried mung beans (also called cellophane noodles) that need to be soaked before being added to stir-fried dishes. When deep-fried, they puff up like a crispy nest. See the recipe for Asian Vegetable Stir-Fry with Crispy Bean Threads on page 56.

Beurre noisette: Literally meaning "hazelnut butter," it's the effect of heating butter gently until it begins to brown and develop a nutty colour and flavour. If the butter is clarified, it will not turn brown.

Blanch: A term I often use, meaning to plunge into rolling, boiling water and semi-cook. When blanching green vegetables, always add salt to retain their vibrant green colour.

Bouquet garni: A classical flavour builder for stocks, soups, etc., usually consisting of thyme sprigs, a bay leaf, parsley, and sometimes a leek green, tied together with twine or wrapped in cheesecloth to enable easy removal before serving.

Brunoise: I love this French culinary term, meaning "cut into very small dice."

Canapé: Literally translated from the French, it means "couch" and refers to any small base of toast, bread, or cracker on which a mousse, garnish, etc., is placed and served as an appetizer.

Caramelize: This can refer to cooking sugar until golden or even slow-cooking onions and other ingredients to gently render their sugar. See the recipe for delicious caramelized apples with buckwheat pancakes on page 168.

Carpaccio: A fairly modern culinary invention of a dish born in northern Italy in the 1960s. Carpaccio should be raw, thinly sliced beef served with a sauce that is slightly acidic, either creamy or with a base of olive oil.

Ceviche (seviche): An old native Latin American combination of seafood that is marinated raw in ample citrus juices and other flavours. The acidity of the juices "cooks" the seafood after marinating for at least 18 hours. It's a great way to keep your kitchen cool for summer entertaining.

Chiffonade: This is one of my favourite culinary terms. It means to roll leaves of herbs or greens like a cigar, then slice them thinly. I often use a chiffonade of basil on pizza or sprinkled on cooked pasta.

Chimichurri: An Argentine herb sauce used as a condiment. It showcases the Italian influence in Argentina, with similarities to Italian salsa verde. The sauce combines cilantro, parsley, garlic, olive oil, and lemon juice, and is drizzled lavishly over grilled beef and empanadas. See the recipe for Grilled Striploin of Beef with Chimichurri on page 132.

Chinoise: A cone-shaped strainer called a China cap in English. It is indispensable in classical cooking for straining soups and sauces.

Chipotle: A dry, smoked, jalapeño chile that should be soaked in hot water to rehydrate it before using. I like to finely chop chipotle (pronounced chi-po-tlay) and add it to sour cream and mayonnaise for extra zip and a smoky flavour. I feature chipotle in the recipes for Grilled Chicken Wrapped in a Tortilla with Chipotle Sour Cream (page 78) and Spicy Shrimp and Corn Chowder (page 98).

Choux paste: A classical French pastry used to make éclairs, cream puffs, and profiteroles. "Choux" is the French word for cabbage, which cream puffs resemble when baked. Take a look at the recipe for Hazelnut Caramel Profiteroles (page 174)—they're to die for.

Cilantro: An herb, also called coriander or Chinese parsley. It seems to be one of those herbs that people either love or have not acquired a taste for. It's an integral part of Thai, Middle Eastern, and Mexican cuisine. If you don't like it, try reducing the quantities rather than abandoning it altogether.

Confit: The French word for preserve. When preserving fruit, the word "confiture" (jam) is used. "Confit" refers to the preparation of preserving anything else. Common examples of confits are duck (cooked and preserved in fat) or onions cooked down to slowly render their sugar.

Coulis: A loose fruit or vegetable sauce, for example, strawberry, raspberry, or tomato. The difference between tomato sauce and a coulis is that the coulis is not cooked. There is a very simple recipe for a tomato coulis drizzled over a cornmeal crusted sea bass on page 113.

Crème fraîche: A rich and tangy heavy cream made popular by the French. In Europe, where cream does not have to be pasteurized, it becomes naturally tangy like yoghurt. In North America a pseudo crème fraîche can be made by adding sour cream, yoghurt, or buttermilk to 35 percent cream and allowing it to thicken slightly. After several days, the cream can be strained through cheesecloth to develop the desired texture.

Deglaze: The term for adding wine, stock, or other liquids to a hot pan to release the pan drippings or crusted bits of flavour left by meats, onions, or other vegetables. The pan can then be returned to heat and you have the base for an accompanying sauce. I use this technique very often.

Dolma: A popular Greek stuffed grapevine leaf. Actually, it's the Arabic word for "something stuffed," but is renowned in Greece. Dolmas or dolmades can be made with cabbage as well and are served hot with an egg lemon sauce or at room temperature stuffed with rice, herbs, and dried fruit.

Drained yoghurt: Yoghurt that has been drained in cheesecloth and that consequently is thicker and richer. If you start with low-fat yoghurt, it's a great low-fat substitute for sour cream. You can use it on potatoes, over fruit, and in cakes. For a classic Greek tzatziki, use a full-fat yoghurt and drain it to get that creamy, thick, village-style yoghurt that's plentiful in Greece (see page 10).

Dredge: To dip in flour, breadcrumbs, or other dry coating before frying. The excess is gently tapped off to ensure a thin layer for an evenly browned crust.

Emulsion: A combination of two liquids that don't normally mix (i.e., oil and water) blended together to form a smooth consistency. Emulsions can be creamy like mayonnaise or hollandaise or they can be vinaigrettes without an emulsifier like egg yolk.

Extra virgin olive oil: The oil extracted from the first cold pressing of the olive. The addition of heat or subsequent pressings yield olive oils that are higher in acid and therefore less fruity. Extra virgin olive oils should not be used at high temperature, as they break down and lose flavour. I use extra virgin olive oil in most of my recipes, but where a recipe calls for frying on high heat or searing, use regular olive oil or blend it with vegetable oil.

French knife: Some people say that I was born with a French knife attached to my hand. What can I say? It's the most useful all-purpose knife ranging in size from 8 to 12 inches. It's great for chopping and slicing, but should not be used to cut bones or other heavy items. Try to find knives that have a bit more carbon steel, as they are easier to keep sharp. I don't recommend the complete carbon steel knives because they stain very quickly.

Grape seed oil: A nutty, unusually flavoured oil great for salads and frying. As you would expect, it's extracted from the seeds of grapes and is primarily composed of polyunsaturated fats. It has a high smoke point, making it great for high-temperature frying.

Hogo: Hogo seems to have originated in Colombia as a flavouring base for cooking rice, soup, and meats. It's a robust blend of onions, olive oil, chicken stock, spices, and tomatoes. When cooked down to a thicker consistency, hogo can be used as a relish or a sauce. See the recipe for Latin Rice and Peas with Chorizo and Mussels on page 103.

Jerk: A spicy Jamaican seasoning or marinade. Traditionally, it's slow-roasted over a pimento-wood fire pit, but today it knows many variations. The key ingredients are scotch bonnet chiles, thyme, allspice, green onions, ginger, garlic, and lime. I have used jerk seasoning to spice up swordfish (page 122), but in Jamaica it's predominately used with pork or chicken.

Julienne: A French culinary term describing thinly cut strips of vegetables. Because I have a classical French culinary background, I often julienne vegetables. See the recipe for sautéed king crab legs with julienne vegetables on page 110.

Kofta: A Middle Eastern term describing ground meats molded into cylindrical shapes and then grilled, fried, or baked. Kofta are very often made of lamb and are fragrantly spiced with cinnamon, allspice, and fresh chopped mint or parsley. Take a look at the recipe for Lamb Kofta with Romesco Sauce on page 145.

Marinate: To soak meats, fish, or vegetables in a flavoured liquid. A marinade almost always contains acid-like citrus or vinegar, so it helps to tenderize tougher cuts of meat. When marinating, do not add salt; this draws out the juices from meats, thereby drying them.

Mince: To chop very finely.

Mirepoix: Pronounced mee-ra-pwah, a mixture of chopped vegetables and herbs used as a flavour base in soups, sauces, and stocks. Usually it consists of onions, celery, carrots, and leeks. If you roast the mirepoix, the flavour will be richer.

Mirin: A sweet Japanese wine made from starchy rice that is low in alcohol. Mirin is great in sauces, soups, and salad dressings.

Mise en place: A term I use over and over again meaning, literally, to put into place. It's the official phrase in the culinary world for having your ingredients chopped and ready for service. An entire chapter is dedicated to mise en place, because cooking will be invigorating if you're organized.

Miso: A Japanese culinary staple made of fermented soy bean paste. It can be purchased at health stores or Japanese specialty shops and is the main ingredient in the famous miso soup. It's high in protein and vitamin B and is a great ingredient for vegetarians. It should be added at the end of cooking or used raw in salad dressings.

Mortar and pestle: A handy grinding implement consisting of a smooth bowl (mortar) and a small rounded stick (pestle), which does the grinding. They can be made of wood, marble, or ceramic and are great for grinding spices. I always use them when I toast my own spices and then grind them to retain all the flavour.

Orecchiette: A pasta shaped like little ears, the translation of the Italian word "orecchiette." I particularly love them because they don't have a consistent thickness; therefore, you always get a crunchy bite at one end. They're also great for holding sauce.

Orzo: Most people think that orzo is rice, but it's actually pasta shaped like an elongated rice grain. It's probably my favourite pasta and it works great in soups or cooked in stock.

Pancetta: An Italian bacon that can be purchased at ethnic supermarkets or butchers. It's not smoked but is a great way to start developing flavour in a sauce, risotto, or soups. I use it quite frequently.

Papillote: "En papillote" describes cooking food in a pouch or envelope. Using parchment paper is the easiest way to enclose foods, keeping in juices. Fish and vegetables are best suited for cooking en papillote.

Pastry bag: Having been a pastry chef for a few years, I can't live without my piping bag. It's a plastic-lined canvas bag that can be fitted with an assortment of tips used for decorating cakes and piping dough and batter, like choux paste. Always wash thoroughly after each use and stand upside down to dry to prevent mold from growing.

Pilaf: Also called pilau, this is a method of cooking rice by browning it first with onions, oil or butter, and garlic and other fragrant spices. The rice is then cooked in stock until the moisture is absorbed.

Purée: To mash cooked food through a food mill, in a food processor or blender, until smooth. After puréeing soups or sauces, they can be strained for an even silkier finish.

Reduce: A common practice in sauce making where a stock, cream, or other flavoured liquid is simmered uncovered. This process allows moisture to evaporate, thereby concentrating the flavour and thickening the liquid. Reduction is the basis for developing flavour in most sauces.

Romesco sauce: A traditional Spanish sauce used to complement grilled meat and poultry. It's a creamy combination of olive oil, almonds, bread, garlic, red pepper, and tomatoes. I have reinvented romesco sauce, pairing it with fragrant lamb kofta (page 145).

Roux: The basic French combination of flour and butter used in countless sauces. The usual ratio of flour to butter is one to one, but the flour can be increased to achieve a thicker sauce. In Cajun cooking, roux gives gumbo its thick texture. If the butter and flour are gently cooked just until blended, the roux will be blond and the sauce will have a delicate flavour. In the case of gumbo, where the fat and flour can be slow-cooked for up to an hour, the resulting roux is dark with an intense, nutty flavour.

Salsa: The Spanish translation of "sauce," salsa is usually made of raw ingredients, generally chunky and served at room temperature. I describe it as a chunky sauce served as a condiment and not cooked into a dish. There are recipes for a couple of different salsas in this book: tomato and black olive (page 115) and citrus papaya (page 110). They are a great, quick, low-fat way to get instant zip.

Sauté: It's pretty rare to prepare one of my recipes without sautéeing something. In French, "sauté" means to jump, which describes the action of the ingredients being tossed quickly over fairly high heat in a pan.

Scallion: Synonymous with spring onion and green onion, an immature onion that is milder in flavour and fully edible. Scallions are great when added at the end of the cooking process to retain their fresh, mild flavour.

Sear: To brown a piece of meat or fish in a very hot, oiled pan, turning to evenly brown all sides. This process reduces the overall cooking time. There is controversy as to whether searing seals in the juices, but I can assure you that it prevents starting the cooking process at low heat, thereby steaming the meat or fish.

Serrated knife: Also known as a bread knife, it's a knife with notches that make cutting bread, tomatoes, and cakes a breeze. The serrated knife keeps its edge longer, but once dull, it should be professionally sharpened.

Sprig: A single stem of a fresh herb. When a recipe calls for a sprig of thyme, this means a loose stem that may have several offshoots attached to it.

Steel: A very useful long rod with a handle, used to keep your knives sharp. The steel realigns the edge on your knife, keeping it sharp. This action should become a regular habit to keep your knives in good working order. It takes a bit of practice, but you will enjoy working with sharp knives. Once a knife becomes dull, the steel is ineffective and you need to graduate to the stone (see below).

Stone: Also know as a whetstone, a rectangular block used to hone a knife's edge. If a knife is honed repeatedly, the stone eventually will eat up its blade. Only use the stone when the steel is ineffective.

Sumac: The dark red berries of a bush that is indigenous to the Middle East and some parts of Italy. It's sold as a dark red powder and has a mild but slightly tangy taste. It can be used in rice, vegetables, meats, and salads.

Sweat: To heat ingredients in a pan very gently in order to soften them. This usually occurs with little or no colouring of the food.

Zest: I think citrus zest is one of the best ways to develop flavour and intensity beyond using citrus juice itself. Zest is the outer skin of all citrus fruits and can be finely grated, julienned, or coarsely chopped. When zesting, be sure to avoid the white pith beneath the outer skin, which tends to be bitter (unless, of course, you are making marmalade).

Sources

Hazan, Marcella. *Marcella's Italian Kitchen*. New York: Alfred A. Knopf, 1993.

Miller, Mark. *The Great Chile Book*. Berkeley: Ten Speed Press, 1991.

Mizer, David A. and Mary Porter. *Food Preparation for the Professional*. London: Harper & Row, 1978.

Palomino, Rafael. *Bistro Latino*. New York: William Morrow and Co. Inc., 1998.

Rodriguez, Douglas. *Nuevo Latino*. Berkeley: 10 Speed Press, 1995.

Tyler Herbst, Sharon. *The New Food Lover's Companion*, 2nd Edition. Barron's Educational Series, 1995.

Willan, Anne. *Complete Guide to Cookery*. London: Dorling Kindersley, 1989.

Mise en Place

Mise en place (pronounced meez-on-plas) means, literally, to put into place (see It's all Greek to Me! for more details). The following are some of my personal tips on getting organized in the kitchen and on achieving the best results when cooking.

recipes

Always read through the entire recipe before cooking. This ensures that you understand the technique and prevents you from jumping the gun and "chopping" all ingredients when they need to be "quartered" or "julienned."

Accompanying each recipe in this book are Options and/or Prep features that provide tips on timing, finding ingredients, variations, and substitutions.

Each recipe is only a guideline, not the declaration of independence. Every cook will execute a recipe slightly differently, so do what suits you best. I always equate it to a musician with a sheet of music in front of him or her. No two violinists will interpret a piece of music in exactly the same way. Similarly, no two cooks will prepare the exact same dish from a recipe. Spontaneity makes cooking fun!

timing

Do as much preparation as you can in advance, especially when entertaining. That is the trick that restaurants use to be able to serve you beautiful food in a relatively short period of time. The secret is to leave only what absolutely has to be done for the last minute (see sidebar). That is called having your mise en place ready. Of course, when you're running in the door and making a salad with your coat still on, you are definitely making the best use of your time—forget the mise en place.

beans

Beans are an incredible ingredient to use because they are low in fat and high in fibre and protein. They do take a bit of extra work, but here is a quick-soaking method that will save you a few hours: Cover the beans in cold water and bring to a boil in a medium pot. Boil for 2 minutes, remove from heat, and let stand for 1 hour. Drain and rinse well in cold water. Cook as described in recipe.

As a last resort, you can use canned beans with some loss of texture and flavour.

Some grocery stores sell frozen beans, which are partially cooked; they are a good compromise between canned and dried beans.

THINGS BEST DONE JUST
BEFORE SERVING

1   Grilling or cooking fish, meat, and poultry

2   Cooking pasta

3   Adding cream or milk to soups

4   Dressing salads

5   Making risotto

6   Grating or slicing potatoes

7   Slicing meat, chicken, or poultry

8   Making whisked or butter-finished sauces

9   Whipping egg whites or cream

10   Stir-frying

greens

Any time you are washing greens, particularly spinach and arugula, make sure you immerse them in a large bowl of cold water. To repeat, lift the greens out of the bowl and transfer them to a second bowl, leaving the sand behind in the bottom of the first bowl. Don't tip the bowl over and drain or sand will go back into the greens.

Always dry greens before serving, preferably in a salad spinner. You can also use a tea towel and gently blot them to absorb the moisture.

When improvising with greens, try not to use too many bitter greens together, as the flavour can be overwhelming.

To maximize storage, wash the greens, pat off excess moisture, wrap in a damp cloth or paper towel, and then wrap in plastic. The softer the green, the more quickly it will spoil.

herbs

A good rule of thumb for herbs is to add robust herbs such as thyme, rosemary, or sage at the beginning of cooking and to add the delicate ones such as basil, parsley, coriander, or chives at the end.

Substitute 1 teaspoon of dried herbs for each tablespoon of fresh herbs that the recipe calls for (alternatively, divide the fresh amount by three when using dried herbs).

The best way to store herbs is lightly wrapped in a damp paper towel within a sealed plastic container. I have kept herbs for as long as two weeks that way. You may want to spray them with a little water from time to time.

potatoes

The potato is a vegetable that can cause you many hours of grief in the kitchen if you don't know what type to use for which purpose.

New potatoes are "immature" potatoes that are small, round, and have thin skins. They are higher in water content and have a waxy texture that is perfect for boiling in potato salad or roasting in the oven. You never want to boil new potatoes and try to mash them unless you are running out of wallpaper glue. The lack of starch turns these taters into a gluey mess when you start stirring them.

Yukon Gold potatoes are the relatively new variety of boiling potatoes that are round and have a golden skin and flesh. These potatoes are the best for mashing since they are a starchy potato, not a waxy one.

Baking potatoes are the long, thicker, darker-skinned mature potatoes with less water and a higher starch content. This makes them ideal for baking or making French fries.

tomatoes

Tomatoes need an entire section of their own because there are so many varieties. But don't treat them as interchangeable (many recipes don't specify what type to use)—each tomato has a special purpose.

tomato sauce

Plum tomatoes are perfect for sauce because they are firm, low in acidity, and have a meatier flesh. Peel them first by immersing them in boiling water for about 8 seconds, then transferring them to cold water. The skin peels right off.

Sauté some onions and garlic in olive oil until soft, about 3 to 5 minutes.

Add 2 large cans of plum tomatoes with juice and some thyme and dried oregano and simmer, uncovered, for about 30 to 60 minutes.

Add fresh basil at the end of the cooking process or it will lose its flavour and colour.

tomato salads

Most large tomatoes are ideal in salads or as garnish. These include the field tomato, the beefsteak tomato, and the round, vine-ripened tomato that has a thicker skin. The higher juice and acidity content of this tomato makes it burst with flavour. Cherry tomatoes are also perfect for salads because they are juicy and sweet.

green tomatoes

The green tomato is not a specific variety, but an underripe field or beefsteak tomato. Simply pick or buy them when they are still green. They are particularly delicious when dipped in cornmeal and pan-fried until crispy.

ingredients

If you use good-quality, fresh ingredients, Mother Nature has already done a lot of the work. If you buy an old piece of fish, you will spend most of your time trying to mask the flavour as opposed to trying to enhance it. Try to use vegetables and fruits in season—they will be cheaper and of a higher quality.

Try to avoid using poor-quality wines in sauces—the only thing worse than drinking a bad glass of wine is concentrating the bad taste in a sauce.

If you've tuned in to *Dish It Out*, you might have heard me say, "Don't get frustrated if you can't find one ingredient in a recipe!" Unless it's the key ingredient, don't spend too much time and energy searching for a specific ingredient. Try the recipe with another spice—what's the worst that can happen?

PREP

- The supreme ruler of tomatoes for sauce is the San Marzano. From a town of the same name in Italy, these tomatoes are farmed on volcanic soil and are renowned worldwide for their incredibly meaty flesh with top-quality flavour. Some upscale specialty stores sell them in cans.

OPTION

- For a richer, sweet sauce, cook it over low heat for a couple of hours. Finally, pass it through a food mill or a processor. Sauce can be frozen or jarred for those cooler months.

pantry

Having a well-stocked pantry is one of the most effective ways you can make your life easier in the kitchen. By gradually adding staples that you can just pull out of your hat in a pinch, you'll find that cooking will be more enjoyable. Most of the recipes in this book are geared to doing just that. See the sidebar for a list of my favourite items to have in the pantry or freezer.

spices

Spices that are seeds should be purchased whole, where possible, to keep their flavour. Store them in a sealed jar and dry-toast them in a small skillet to give them a nutty taste. Use a mortar and pestle to grind them just before adding to a recipe. You can also wrap seeds in a tea towel and pound with a rolling pin to grind. Another good trick is to have two coffee grinders: one for coffee beans and one to grind spices.

Always, always, always use freshly ground black peppercorns, not store-bought ground pepper, which has little or no flavour! It's about time that everyone puts a pepper mill on the kitchen countertop.

Nutmeg should be bought whole, stored in an airtight container, and grated as needed.

Personally, I'm not fond of the taste of white pepper and don't follow the classical rule that white sauces should contain white pepper so you don't see the flecks. I think if it's going to have pepper, you should see it. Ultimately, the choice is yours.

To round out this introductory chapter, I thought you might appreciate some basic recipes that you will be using over and over again.

USEFUL PANTRY ITEMS

1   Stock (preferably fresh)—recipes follow on pages 6 to 9, but frozen or canned stock is an alternative

2   Canned tomatoes (the best quality plum tomatoes possible)

3   Tomato paste (in a tube is much easier to store and use)

4   Extra virgin olive oil (gives you instant flavour)

5   Basmati rice (cooks in 12 minutes and is quite fragrant without much help)

6   Tamari (good-quality soy sauce doesn't taste just like salt and gives great flavour)

7   Coconut milk (great for curries or cooking rice, but use in moderation: it isn't low in fat)

8   Chipotles (smoked and dried jalapeño chiles; they add intense flavour to many dishes)

9   Balsamic vinegar (great in salads and on vegetables)

10 Rice wine vinegar (a smoother-tasting vinegar, also great in dressings and sauces)

11 Black sesame seeds (delicious as a crust on chicken or fish or just sprinkled on salads)

12 Clam juice (a quick alternative to fish stock)

Stock

- Traditionally, the bouquet garni is wrapped in cheesecloth and tied with twine for easy retrieval. When I'm in a hurry I simply toss all the ingredients in, since I know I will be straining it through a fine sieve anyway. I've added a rosemary sprig, which is not customary. Do not add too much rosemary or it will become rosemary stock.

- If you want to use the stock right after making it, try to pour it into several shallow baking pans so it cools quickly. You don't want to have the stock at a warm temperature for too long because bacteria love that. Place in freezer so that the fat congeals on top and you can scrape it off. Run a paper towel across the top of the stock to remove any excess fat. Chill until ready to use.

- Never use lean meat for stock; it is the bones with marrow and gelatin that provide all the flavour and texture.

Stock is the fundamental base of most soups and sauces. It can be made from veal, chicken, beef, duck, fish, or even vegetables. I am aware that we have less and less time these days, but homemade stock adds so much flavour to just about anything. It's a great Sunday afternoon project to involve the whole family in and it can be made in huge amounts, portioned into plastic containers, and frozen for everyday use. The second-best option is to use the frozen stock that many grocers are carrying these days. The last resort is canned, but go for labels that say broth. When you use canned stock, never add salt to the soup or sauce because when reduced, the salt in canned stock becomes highly concentrated and will be hard to remedy.

chicken stock

I consider chicken stock to be the most versatile stock. It is flavourful enough to work in sauces, soups, or pasta broth but does not wield the same power as beef or duck stock. It also can be used in vegetable preparations, except when cooking for vegetarians. Nothing is as soothing as chicken noodle soup made from homemade chicken stock.

3-4 lb	raw chicken backs, feet, and necks	*1.4-1.8 kg*
2	large onions, coarsely chopped	*2*
2	large carrots, coarsely chopped	*2*
2	stalks celery, coarsely chopped	*2*
3	whole cloves of garlic, peeled	*3*
1	leek, well cleaned and coarsely chopped (optional)	*1*
16 cups	cold water	*4 L*

Bouquet garni

4	sprigs fresh thyme	*4*
3	parsley stems	*3*
1	sprig rosemary	*1*
1 tsp	whole peppercorns, about 8	*5 mL*
1	whole clove (optional)	*1*
2	bay leaves	*2*

Rinse chicken bones well in cold water. Transfer to a large stockpot—at least 8 L (2 gallons)—and add vegetables and bouquet garni. Cover with cold water and bring to a boil over heat.

When liquid just comes to a boil, skim off the scum that floats on top and immediately reduce heat to a very low simmer. Water should be simmering but not bubbling too rapidly or stock will cloud. It is very important for water to reach the boiling point first or the stock will never reach the proper temperature.

Simmer uncovered for at least 2 hours or up to 5 hours if you want more concentrated flavour. Strain the stock through a fine sieve and cool. Store in small containers in freezer until ready to use. Skim fat off top before using.

Makes about 3 L (12 cups), depending on how long stock is simmered.

fish stock

Unlike chicken or meat stock, fish stock should only be simmered for exactly 20 minutes or it begins to go bitter. It's quicker than you thought, right? You also should make sure the fish heads and bones you use are fresh and run through cold water to remove any blood that will cloud the stock. Fish stock is great for soups, reduced white wine sauces, as a pasta sauce, or in seafood risotto.

3 lbs	fresh fish heads and carcasses	*1.4 kg*
2	medium onions, coarsely chopped	*2*
1	small carrot, cut into 1-in/2.5-cm pieces	*1*
2	stalks celery, coarsely chopped	*2*
1	leek, white part only, washed and coarsely chopped	*1*
1-1/2 cups	dry white wine	*375 mL*
10 cups	cold water	*2.5 L*

Bouquet garni

3	sprigs fresh thyme	*3*
3	stems fresh parsley	*3*
2	bay leaves	*2*
1	whole clove (optional)	*1*
12	whole peppercorns	*12*

OPTIONS

- For a quick brown chicken stock, take the leftover carcass and pan drippings of a roasted chicken, cover with cold water, vegetables, and bouquet garni, and simmer on low for about 1 to 2 hours or until flavour is to your liking.

- Recipe can be doubled easily, as long as you have a gigantic stockpot.

PREP

- The key to great fish stock is using the proper bones and cooking for only 20 minutes. Ask your fishmonger for white, lean fish and avoid using oily fish or freshwater fish like trout.

- You will get maximum flavour if the bones are gently scored with a cleaver to release the inner flavour of the bone before cooking.

OPTION

- The quickest substitute for fish stock is clam juice, which you will find makes a great addition to your pantry.

Rinse the fish bones very well under cold water, removing all traces of blood, especially in gills. Transfer to a large stockpot and add all other ingredients. Bring to a boil over high heat, skim off top foam, and immediately reduce heat to low and simmer uncovered at a gentle boil for exactly 20 minutes.

Strain immediately and cool. Stock can be used immediately since it contains only trace fat. Makes about 2.5 L (10 cups).

brown stock

Brown stock can be made from a variety of bones, but I like using beef or veal. Veal bones yield a more delicate flavour. Brown stocks are the basis for many sauces in restaurants that give pronounced flavour when reduced. They are also perfect for low-fat cooking since they add good body without all the fat. The main difference between brown and light stocks is that you roast the bones in the oven before transferring them to a pot to simmer. This is what provides that dark colour and intensifies the flavour.

2 tsp	vegetable oil	*10 mL*
3 lbs	beef or veal bones, cut or cracked by butcher	*1.4 kg*
2	onions, cut into 8 sections each	*2*
2	carrots, cut into 1-in/2.5-cm pieces	*2*
2	stalks celery, cut into 1-in/2.5-cm pieces	*2*
1	large leek, washed and cut into thick slices	*1*
6	whole cloves garlic, peeled	*6*
3 tbsp	tomato paste (optional)	*45 mL*
1-1/2 cups	dry red wine	*375 mL*
16 cups	cold water	*4 L*

Bouquet garni

3	sprigs thyme	*3*
2	sprigs rosemary	*2*
3	parsley stems	*3*
10	whole peppercorns	*10*
1	bay leaf	*1*
2	whole cloves (optional)	*2*

PREP

- It is best to transfer strained stock into shallow pans to cool quickly in fridge. Skim off fat once stock has cooled and keep in fridge for a couple of days or freeze.
- If you opt not to add tomato paste, your stock will have less colour and intensity.

OPTION

- You can use 500 mL (2 cups) of this stock at a time and simmer to reduce by one half. This will make great sauces, broth for pasta, or risotto.

Preheat oven to 230°C (450°F). Pour oil into a large roasting pan. Add bones and roast in lower rack of oven for about 20 to 30 minutes or until golden. Stir often to ensure even browning.

Add vegetables and bouquet garni and continue to roast for about 15 minutes or until vegetables begin to turn golden. Add tomato paste and red wine and stir well.

Transfer to a large stockpot and cover with cold water. Use a little water to fully deglaze the roasting pan to get maximum flavour.

Bring to a boil over high heat and skim fat off the top with a slotted spoon. As soon as stock begins to boil, reduce heat to a gentle simmer. Simmer for 2-1/2 to 5 hours, depending on your schedule.

Strain the stock through a fine sieve and chill as rapidly as possible. Store in small containers in freezer until ready to use. Skim fat off top before using.

Makes about 2 L (8 cups), depending on how long stock is simmered.

Tzatziki (Greek Yoghurt Garlic Dip)

PREP

- If you're in a rush, you can always buy drained yoghurt at specialty Greek shops. If you don't drain the yoghurt, the tzatziki will be loose.

OPTIONS

- For a lower-fat version, use low-fat yoghurt and drain it a little longer.
- To make the Indian version of this, called "raita," don't drain the yoghurt, reduce the garlic by half, and dice the cucumber instead of grating it.

Once you know how to pronounce this one, the rest is a breeze. Most Greeks like the garlic to be in the stratosphere, but I prefer it a little more subtle. This is a great dip for veggies and bread, or a good sauce for meats and chicken.

2 cups	whole-milk yoghurt	*500 mL*
1	large English cucumber, peeled and grated	*1*
2-3	cloves garlic, minced	*2-3*
	Salt and pepper, to taste	
	Chopped fresh mint (optional)	

Line a colander or sieve with cheesecloth and place it over a bowl. Add yoghurt and allow it to drain in fridge for 2 hours or more. In medium bowl, combine drained yoghurt with cucumber and garlic. Season to taste and add chopped mint, if desired.

Makes about 375 mL (1-1/2 cups).

Aïoli

This classic garlic mayonnaise comes from the south of France. It's pronounced "i-ee-o-ly" and the French use it on everything from sandwiches to French fries. I'm adding a pinch of saffron, but you can leave that out if you like.

2-3	cloves garlic, chopped	*2-3*
1/4 tsp	salt	*1 mL*
1	egg yolk	*1*
	Juice of 1/2 lemon	
Pinch	saffron	*Pinch*
1/2 tsp	cayenne	*2 mL*
1/2 cup	olive oil	*125 mL*

Crush garlic cloves and place in food processor. Add salt, egg yolk, lemon juice, saffron, and cayenne. Pulse machine to combine ingredients. In a steady stream add olive oil slowly through spout with machine on until mixture is smooth.

Makes about 125 mL (1/2 cup).

Mango Salsa

I developed this simple salsa to be served with a grilled piece of citrus salmon. It would be ideal for swordfish, rainbow trout, or chicken. It's colourful, bursting with citrus, and easy to make.

1	each red pepper and medium red onion, finely diced	1
	Juice of 1 lime and 1/2 orange	
1	large mango, diced	1
1 tbsp	chopped fresh coriander	15 mL
1/2	small chile, finely chopped	1/2

Combine all ingredients in small bowl and allow flavours to develop for a few hours.

Serve over chicken or fish.

Makes 4 to 6 servings.

OPTIONS

- For salsa that is a little creamy, purée half the ingredients and add them back to the chopped ones.
- Use papaya or pineapple instead of mango.

Christine's
All-Purpose BBQ Sauce

Balsamic vinegar and apple butter give this sauce a tangy bite. It is perfect for almost anything that needs a barbecue sauce, and is fabulous on ribs and wings. BBQ sauces are usually a balance of sugar and acidity, so if you omit an ingredient, try to balance by omitting a little of the opposite flavour. In other words, if you are leaving out the honey, you may want to reduce the lemon juice a bit.

• For a smoky flavour, use chipotle chiles or any other smoked chile.

• If you don't like the spice, simply eliminate the cayenne pepper.

2	large cloves garlic, minced	2
2 tbsp	balsamic vinegar	30 mL
1 tsp	Worcestershire sauce	5 mL
2 tbsp	soy sauce	30 mL
1 tsp	honey	5 mL
	Juice of 1/2 lemon	
3 tbsp	ketchup	45 mL
1/3 cup	tomato juice	75 mL
2 tbsp	brown sugar	30 mL
1 tsp	Dijon mustard	5 mL
1/4 cup	apple juice	50 mL
2 tbsp	apple butter (optional)	30 mL
1/2 tsp	cayenne pepper	2 mL
1 tsp	paprika	5 mL
1/2	dried chile, chopped	1/2
	Salt and pepper, to taste	

Combine all ingredients together in a medium bowl and stir until well blended. Use on chicken, ribs, or burgers.

Makes about 325 mL (1-1/3 cups).

For Starters

New Potato, Artichoke, and Assorted Bean Salad

**Serves 4 to 6
as a side dish**

PREP

- To prepare artichokes, remove about one-third of the outer leaves and trim the artichoke's pointed end, cutting off about 2.5 cm (1 in). Trim the base with a peeler or small, serrated paring knife, removing all tough outer skin. Cut artichokes in quarters and rub immediately with lemon juice.

- This salad can be made the day before and kept in the fridge, and is perfect for a picnic lunch.

OPTIONS

- Low-fat cooks can reduce olive oil to 15 mL (1 tbsp), add 15 mL (1 tbsp) Dijon mustard instead of dry mustard, and reduce lemon juice by half. Use the best olive oil for maximum taste.

- Substitute red tomatoes and yellow peppers.

- Eliminate the artichokes.

This is a great spring or summer salad that can be as simple as you make it. If you're a perfectionist, you will probably want to use dried beans and fresh artichokes, which take longer to prepare. If you are in a bind, you can use marinated artichokes and canned beans and the salad is a snap. This salad also provides a good opportunity to introduce the family to artichokes, if you have not yet done so. It makes a great side dish to simple grilled chicken and fish, or an ideal vegetarian main dish.

1 cup	assorted dried beans, or 1 10-oz/284-g can	*250 mL*
4	medium artichokes (or jarred artichokes)	*4*
	Juice of 1 lemon	
3 tbsp	red wine vinegar	*45 mL*
1 tbsp	dry mustard	*15 mL*
2	medium new potatoes, scrubbed and whole with skin on	*2*
1	red pepper, chopped	*1*
1	medium red onion, chopped	*1*
1	medium yellow tomato, cut into wedges	*1*
1/4 cup	olive oil	*50 mL*
1 tsp	chopped fresh coriander	*5 mL*
1 tbsp	each chopped fresh parsley and chopped fresh chives	*15 mL*
	Salt and freshly cracked black pepper, to taste	

Soak beans overnight in medium bowl full of cold water. Drain and cook in salted water over medium heat until tender, about 45 minutes. Drain and set aside.

Clean and quarter artichokes and rub immediately with lemon juice to prevent browning. Poach over low heat in water until tender, about 15 to 18 minutes. Remove from water. Remove fluffy pink middle and discard.

Combine vinegar and dry mustard in a small bowl and whisk until blended.

In another pot, cover potatoes in cold, salted water. Cook until tender, about 18 to 20 minutes, and drain. Slice while still warm and drizzle with half of the vinegar mixture.

Combine cooked or canned beans with artichokes, potatoes, and remaining ingredients. Toss only to blend, as potatoes and artichokes are very delicate.

Endive, Spinach, and Grapefruit Salad

Serves 6

Blood oranges can easily add sophistication to a simple salad dressing. Since they are only available from about November to March, see the option for the dressing. This unique fruit is native to Italy and is a radiant orange with a tangy bite and subtle sugar. The addition of the grapefruit makes it a true winter salad. If you find that the endive is a little too bitter, use spinach instead.

1	head Belgian endive, trimmed, with leaves separated	*1*
1	small bunch spinach, leaves only	*1*
1	large ruby red grapefruit, sectioned	*1*
1/4 cup	pecans, chopped	*50 mL*

Dressing

2	shallots, chopped	*2*
1/4 cup	canola oil	*50 mL*
3/4 cup	blood orange juice	*175 mL*
2 tbsp	rice wine vinegar	*30 mL*
	Salt and pepper	

Cut bottom stem off endive. Chop and set aside.

Rinse spinach thoroughly several times to remove the dirt. Break into small pieces with hands. Spin dry. Combine the greens in a medium bowl.

Sauté the shallots in 15 mL (1 tbsp) of canola oil for about 3 minutes, or until soft. Meanwhile, heat the blood orange juice in a small saucepan and simmer on low until reduced to 125 mL (1/2 cup). Remove from heat and combine with the shallots. Add vinegar and remaining oil and whisk vigorously. Season with salt and pepper to taste.

Pour dressing over greens and toss well. Add grapefruit sections and pecans and toss.

PREP
- Belgian endive is quite fragile, so prepare it just before serving.
- Dressing can be made in advance and keeps for several days in fridge.

OPTIONS
- Mesclun mix can be used as a quick substitute for spinach and endive. By adding different dressings the mix can be unique every time.
- Substitute 125 mL (1/2 cup) orange juice and 50 mL (1/4 cup) grapefruit juice for the blood orange juice.

Grilled Vegetable Salad

Serves 4 to 6

Here's a versatile summer salad that can be served hot or cold. You can use just about any vegetable that strikes your fancy, not only the ones that I suggest. Served with some fresh crusty bread, this salad makes a great lunch or it can play second fiddle to your main event. In the winter, you can choose seasonal vegetables and roast them instead of using the barbecue. How's that for flexibility?

2	baby eggplant (or 1 small Sicilian eggplant)	2
2	medium zucchini	2
1	red pepper	1
1	yellow pepper	1
1/4 cup	olive oil	50 mL
3 tbsp	balsamic vinegar	45 mL
1	large clove garlic, chopped	1
1/4 cup	chopped fresh basil	50 mL
1	medium red onion, chopped	1
2	medium field or vine-ripened tomatoes, cut into wedges	2
1/4 cup	black olives (optional)	50 mL
1/4 cup	crumbled goat cheese (optional)	50 mL
	Salt and freshly cracked black pepper	

PREP

- You need to put a little bit of muscle into this one at the beginning, but it keeps well in the fridge. It's best when served at room temperature.
- This is a great picnic or potluck recipe.
- Toss any leftover salad into freshly cooked pasta.

OPTION

- To give this salad a Greek feel, use feta cheese instead of goat cheese.

Slice eggplant lengthwise into 5-mm (1/4-in) slices and sprinkle with salt. Place on a wire rack and allow bitter juices to bleed for about 30 minutes. Rinse off salt and pat dry.

Slice zucchini diagonally into 5-mm (1/4-in) slices. Core peppers and cut into 4 equal rectangles. Cut each rectangle into 2 triangles. In a medium bowl, mix olive oil, balsamic vinegar, garlic, black pepper to taste, and basil. Add all vegetables, except onions and tomatoes, and toss.

Heat grill or barbecue and rub with an oiled cloth to prevent sticking. Grill vegetables for about 3 minutes on each side. Put vegetables back into bowl with oil mixture and add onions and tomatoes. If desired, sprinkle with black olives and goat cheese before serving.

Nappa and Carrot Slaw with Lemongrass Ginger Dressing

Serves 6 to 8

Why not try an interesting, very flavourful variation on coleslaw? Not only is this salad easy to make, but it is so much more delicious than regular coleslaw. On the show, I served it with a simple grilled rainbow trout, but you can serve it with just about any grilled meat, fish, or chicken. The combination of ginger and lemongrass makes it perfect with Asian stir-fries. It would be particularly mouthwatering in the summer. Don't be shocked by the simple directions—you're not missing anything.

1	head small nappa cabbage, core removed and finely sliced	1
3	large carrots, peeled and grated	3
1/4 cup	finely chopped chives	50 mL

Dressing

1 tsp	grated fresh ginger	5 mL
1	stalk lemongrass, only inner white part, finely minced	1
1/2 tsp	Dijon mustard	2 mL
4 tbsp	rice wine vinegar	60 mL
5 tbsp	grape seed oil	75 mL
	Salt and pepper, to taste	

In a large bowl, whisk together all ingredients for dressing. Add cabbage, carrots, and chives. Toss well to combine. Cover and refrigerate for at least 1 hour before serving.

PREP

- Lemongrass is stringy, so you need to mince it as finely as you can with a heavy, sharp knife.

- If you're in a hurry, make the salad portion only and use it as a bed for grilled fish or chicken. The warmth of the fish or chicken will slightly wilt the cabbage, giving it better flavour without having to let it sit.

- This salad is a great item for a lunch buffet because it keeps beautifully at room temperature.

OPTIONS

- If you don't have, or don't want to use, lemongrass, substitute the zest of 1 lemon.

- You can use canola oil in place of grape seed oil, but the flavour will not be nutty.

Red Oak Leaf and Boston Salad with Toasted Pumpkin Seeds

Serves 6

Since I am the reigning queen of options, I want you to know that you can use any kind of lettuce that you prefer for this recipe. It makes a great salad for the fall season, with the pumpkin seeds and apple cider vinegar, but you can serve it just about any time of the year. This salad is like that simple black shirt that goes with just about anything and doesn't need to be dry-cleaned.

1	head small red oak leaf lettuce	*1*
1	head small Boston bibb lettuce	*1*
1/2 cup	pumpkin seeds	*125 mL*

Dressing

1	shallot, minced	*1*
1/4 cup	apple cider vinegar	*50 mL*
1/4 cup	buttermilk	*50 mL*
1/4 cup	canola oil	*50 mL*
1 tsp	honey	*5 mL*
1 tsp	Dijon mustard	*5 mL*
	Salt and pepper, to taste	

PREP

• You can buy toasted pumpkin seeds, if you don't want to toast them yourself.

OPTIONS

• For a very low-fat version of this salad, reduce the oil to 15 mL (1 tbsp), increase the buttermilk to 75 mL (1/3 cup), and reduce the vinegar to 30 mL (2 tbsp).

• Sunflower seeds can be substituted for the pumpkin seeds.

Wash lettuce and tear with hands. Spin dry and reserve.

Toast pumpkin seeds in oven at 180°C (350°F) for 5 to 8 minutes, or until golden. Remove and reserve.

Combine all ingredients for dressing in food processor and pulse several times until smooth. Adjust seasoning.

Toss salad in dressing and sprinkle with seeds before serving.

Red Lentil and Apple Salad

The combination of cooked red lentils and crisp raw apples gives this salad a unique texture. And the mixture of cinnamon, cumin, and apple cider vinegar provides a spicy yet sweet pairing. This salad also features a low-fat content that's ideal for vegetarians and other health-conscious cooks, and it can be made in about 15 minutes.

Serves 4

2 tbsp	olive oil	*30 mL*
1	small onion, diced	*1*
1/2 tsp	good-quality hot curry powder	*2 mL*
1 tsp	cumin seed, ground	*5 mL*
1 cup	red lentils, washed and picked over	*250 mL*
1	cinnamon stick	*1*
1-3/4 cups	water	*425 mL*
1	McIntosh apple, diced	*1*
2 tbsp	apple cider vinegar	*30 mL*
	Salt and pepper, to taste	

In a medium saucepan, sauté onion, curry powder, and cumin in olive oil for 3 to 5 minutes, or until onion is soft. Add lentils, cinnamon stick, and water. Bring to a boil, reduce heat to medium, and cook, uncovered, for about 10 minutes, or until lentils are tender and moisture has evaporated. Transfer to a baking sheet and cool slightly.

Discard cinnamon stick and combine with apple and vinegar in a medium bowl. Season with salt and pepper and toss well.

Serve at room temperature.

PREP

- When picking over lentils, look for little pebbles that may do tooth damage if undetected. Discard them and rinse lentils before cooking.
- This salad can be made in advance and refrigerated for a few days.
- Great for room-temperature buffets and for vegetarians.

OPTIONS

- You can easily add some roasted, diced sweet potato to make this salad a vegetarian main course.
- Granny Smith apples will give the dish a tangy edge.

Potato-Crusted Scallops with Avocado Tomato Salad

Serves 4

"Chic" is a word that came to mind when I developed this interesting appetizer. I created it one evening when I invited my producer over for dinner. It was such a success that I thought I'd share it with you. It's a little more challenging than my everyday fare, but still very easy to master. It's just the thing for a gathering of special friends. The ingredients are all very easy to find—it's the combination of crisp potato encrusting the delicate scallops that is unusual.

PREP

- Make sure you prepare the salad first, then cover and chill it while you work on the potato rounds.
- All other ingredients should be chopped first, as potatoes will discolour quickly after grating.
- Potato rounds can be fried until golden on both sides and then transferred to a baking sheet. Just before serving, warm them in a hot oven.

OPTIONS

- To simplify, eliminate the potato rounds and simply sear the scallops, whole, in a skillet and serve the same way over the salad.
- Scallops also can be grilled and served over salad in summer.

Salad

1	each ripe avocado and large vine-ripened or field tomato, diced	1
1	small yellow pepper, finely diced	1
3 tbsp	extra virgin olive oil	45 mL
1/2 tsp	Dijon mustard	2 mL
	Juice of 1/2 lemon	
	Salt and freshly cracked black pepper, to taste	
	Fresh coriander, chopped (optional)	
	Sour cream or yoghurt (optional)	

Scallops

2	green onions, finely chopped	2
1 tsp	chopped fresh dill	5 mL
2	Yukon gold potatoes, peeled and grated	2
	Salt and pepper, to taste	
4	medium scallops, sliced into thirds crosswise	4
2 tbsp	vegetable oil	30 mL

In medium bowl, combine avocado, tomato, and yellow pepper. Toss. In small bowl, whisk together olive oil, mustard, and lemon juice until combined. Add to avocado mixture and toss. Season with salt and pepper and add coriander, if desired. Cover and set aside until scallops are cooked.

Combine onion, dill, and potato in small bowl and stir to mix. Season with salt and pepper. Season scallops with salt and pepper.

Heat vegetable oil in medium-sized skillet over medium heat. Spread about 15 mL (1 tbsp) of potato mixture at a time in the skillet, a little larger than the width of scallop. Lay a slice of scallop on top of potato mixture and cover with an equal amount of potato mixture. Press down firmly with spatula and fry for 3 minutes per side, or until potatoes are brown and crisp. Work with 4 potato rounds at a time. Repeat with remaining scallop slices until all are cooked. Drain on paper towel to absorb extra oil.

Divide salad among 4 plates and place 3 potato rounds on top of each. Drizzle with yoghurt or sour cream, if desired.

Arugula, Tomato, and Shaved Asiago Salad

Serves 6

Arugula is a delicious peppery green that is quite delicate, but loaded with flavour. I highly recommend tomato salads in the summer, since tomatoes then are sweet, luscious, and have a perfect balance of sugar and acidity. Asiago is a creamy relative to Parmesan and is just the thing to round out the peppery zip of the greens.

2	bunches arugula	2
6	medium tomatoes, field or vine ripened	6
4 oz	Asiago cheese	114 g

Dressing

1/4 cup	brandy or sherry vinegar	50 mL
1/3 cup	extra virgin olive oil	75 mL
1 tsp	Dijon mustard	5 mL
1 tbsp	sugar	15 mL
	Salt and pepper, to taste	

PREP

- All components of salad can be prepared in advance and kept separately and covered in the fridge for up to 2 days. The arugula will be the first to wilt.

OPTIONS

- Substitute spinach for the arugula.
- Substitute Parmesan for the Asiago.

Wash arugula well to remove sand, and trim stems. Dry in salad spinner or with tea towel. Cut tomatoes into wedges and shave cheese. Combine arugula, tomatoes, and cheese, saving some cheese for garnish. Toss salad in dressing and garnish with cheese.

Rice Noodle Salad
with Red Peppers and Cashews

Serves 6 to 8

This is probably the best noodle salad for those of you tired of, or intolerant to, wheat noodles. The salad is best served at room temperature and makes a very simple side dish to any stir-fry. It's also a good alternative to rice and has minimal fat. Even the kids will probably enjoy it since it looks like a noodle. The salad requires little or no assembly; that is, it's very easy to put together!

PREP
- If you want the cashews to keep their crunch, add them just before serving the salad.
- Very thin rice noodles should not be boiled, as they tend to become sticky.
- When served too cold, the salad will lose some of its flavour.

OPTIONS
- Some pan-fried tofu can be added to this salad for vegetarians.
- Substitute peanuts for the cashews.
- In summer, add some grilled chicken or grilled shrimp for added intensity and to make this salad a meal.

1/2 lb	vermicelli rice noodles	*227 g*
1/4 cup	soy sauce	*50 mL*
1 tsp	grated fresh ginger	*5 mL*
3	green onions, finely chopped	*3*
2	carrots, julienned	*2*
1	red pepper, cut into thin strips	*1*
1	small chile pepper, finely chopped	*1*
1/4 cup	rice wine vinegar	*50 mL*
1 tsp	sesame oil	*5 mL*
1 tbsp	canola oil	*15 mL*
1/4 cup	salted, roasted cashews	*50 mL*

Soak rice noodles in very hot, but not boiling, water. Set aside for 30 minutes. Drain well to remove excess water. Meanwhile, combine remaining ingredients in medium bowl and stir well. Add noodles and toss several times to combine well.

Spinach and Arugula Salad with Roasted Pepper Dressing

Serves 4 to 6

The dressing for this salad is what makes it so special. Adding the roasted yellow pepper gives the whole salad a sweet balance and vibrant yellow colour. Spinach and arugula has always been one of my favourite combinations, since one is sweet and the other is peppery, but topped with this simple dressing they are amazing.

1	bunch arugula	*1*
1	small bunch spinach, stems removed	*1*
1	small red onion, sliced	*1*

Dressing

1	yellow pepper	*1*
1/3 cup	extra virgin olive oil	*75 mL*
1/4 cup	apple cider vinegar	*50 mL*
1 tsp	Dijon mustard	*5 mL*
1 tsp	sugar	*5 mL*
	Salt and freshly ground pepper, to taste	

Wash all greens in deep, cold water. Drain water and repeat until no sand is found in sink. Spin to remove excess water.

Preheat oven to 190°C (375°F).

Roast whole pepper on middle rack of oven for 20 to 25 minutes, or until browned, turning often. Remove and place in paper bag to sweat for 5 minutes. Peel skin from pepper. Remove seeds and purée in food processor.

Add remaining ingredients for dressing and pulse until smooth.

Combine greens and onion. Toss salad in half the dressing and serve. Reserve remaining dressing to drizzle on top.

PREP

- Yellow peppers can be roasted and peeled in advance and kept in oil for a couple of days in the fridge. Immersing the peppers in cold water is a quick way of removing the skin, but you lose the flavour that the water washes away.

- If dressing begins to separate before serving, transfer back to food processor and pulse until blended.

OPTIONS

- Substitute any kind of vegetable oil for olive oil.

- Use roasted red peppers instead of yellow.

- If you can't find arugula, double the spinach.

Sautéed Shrimp and Endive Salad

Serves 4 to 6

Although this recipe falls into the salad category, it's really a miniature meal. Serve it as a full lunch or as a simple appetizer for a pasta main course. Remember one rule of thumb in menu planning: If your appetizer contains seafood, your main course should not. I was definitely in a Mediterranean mood when I combined these tastes from Spain and France to show you that everyday cooking does not have to be boring!

1/4 cup	olive oil	*50 mL*
1/2 lb	large tiger shrimp, peeled and deveined	*227 g*
	Several threads saffron	
	Salt and pepper	
2	cloves garlic, chopped	*2*
1/4 cup	dry white wine	*50 mL*
2	plum tomatoes, diced	*2*
	Juice of 1 orange	
4	fresh sprigs parsley, chopped	*4*
1/4 cup	sherry vinegar	*50 mL*
3-4	heads Belgian endive, cleaned and trimmed	*3-4*
1	red pepper, diced	*1*
1	orange, segmented	*1*

Heat half of olive oil in skillet on high. Add shrimp, saffron, and a little salt and pepper. Sauté for 2 minutes, or until shrimp are just translucent. Remove from heat and remove shrimp from pan and reserve. Add garlic and sauté for 1 minute. Add wine and tomatoes and cover. Reduce heat to medium and simmer for 3 minutes, until tomatoes are just soft. Return shrimp to pan to heat through, about 1 minute.

Whisk together remaining olive oil, orange juice, parsley, and vinegar. Season with salt and pepper. Pour dressing over endive and toss with red pepper and orange segments. Spoon warm shrimp mixture over tossed salad.

PREP

- In summer, I would grill my shrimp before adding them to the salad.
- If you want to peel your tomatoes, simply immerse them in boiling water for 10 seconds, then plunge them immediately into cold water. Peel the skins off and proceed with the recipe.

OPTIONS

- The best substitute for sherry vinegar is red wine vinegar, to which you could add a splash of sherry just for fun.
- Use a sturdy leaf lettuce in place of the endive in a pinch (escarole is ideal).

Strawberry, Radicchio, and Endive Salad

Serves 4 to 6

I would be inclined to make this salad in summer at the peak of strawberry season. That may sound like I'm fencing you in, but that's when you will get the optimum taste from the strawberries. The blend of balsamic and rice wine vinegar gives you just enough sweet intensity with a tart finish.

1	small head of radicchio, washed	*1*
1	head endive, washed, trimmed, and sliced	*1*
1 pint	strawberries, hulled, stemmed, and quartered	*475 mL*
1/4 cup	walnuts	*50 mL*

Dressing

1	shallot, minced	*1*
2 tbsp	rice wine vinegar	*30 mL*
2 tbsp	balsamic vinegar	*30 mL*
2 tbsp	canola oil	*30 mL*
3 tbsp	olive oil	*45 mL*
	Freshly cracked black pepper, to taste	

Dry greens in spinner or with a tea towel. Combine greens and strawberries and toss to mix.

Combine all ingredients for dressing in a food processor and pulse until smooth. Adjust seasoning. Toss greens with half the dressing. If salad seems too dry, add more dressing. Sprinkle with walnuts. Reserve any leftover dressing for pouring over top of salad, if desired.

PREP

• Once you have washed your strawberries, they should be used quickly. Water seems to make them mushy in a hurry.

OPTIONS

• For a completely different texture, purée half of the strawberries in the dressing. Use the rest as per recipe.

• If endive or radicchio is not your thing, use a firm green lettuce in its place.

Christine's Caesar Salad

Serves 4 to 6

Any authentic Caesar dressing contains a raw egg yolk; as long as you use fresh egg yolks kept cold in the fridge you should be all right. Since there's no guarantee, I leave it entirely up to you. Always keep the eggs cold, use the dressing right away, and don't let the salad stand at room temperature.

1	head romaine lettuce, washed, trimmed, and torn in pieces	1

Dressing

2	cloves garlic, minced	2
1/2 tsp	each Dijon mustard and anchovy paste	2 mL
Dash	Worcestershire sauce	Dash
2	drops Tabasco sauce	2
	Juice of 1/2 lemon	
2 tbsp	red wine vinegar	30 mL
	Freshly cracked black pepper, to taste	
1	egg yolk	1
1/3 cup	extra virgin olive oil	75 mL
2 tbsp	grated Parmesan cheese	30 mL

Croutons

2	slices baguette, cut into 1/2-in/1-cm cubes	2
2 tbsp	extra virgin olive oil	30 mL
1	clove garlic, minced	1

Combine all ingredients for dressing, except oil and Parmesan, in food processor and pulse until smooth. In a steady stream, pour in oil while processor is on. Add half of Parmesan and adjust seasoning. Set aside.

Preheat oven to 190°C (375°F). Toss bread cubes with olive oil and garlic until combined. Spread on baking sheet and toast in oven for 6 to 8 minutes, or until golden. Remove from oven and cool.

To assemble salad, spin lettuce until dry. Toss in bowl with dressing and sprinkle with croutons. Toss until well combined. Sprinkle with remaining Parmesan, if desired.

PREP
- The dressing should be used immediately.
- If you opt to eliminate the egg yolk, the dressing can be stored in the fridge in a covered container for several days. Give it a good shake before serving.

OPTIONS
- The extra virgin olive oil gives a strong, full flavour to the dressing; you may want to use a regular olive oil or half olive oil and half canola oil.
- Parmesan cheese can be shaved and sprinkled on top of lettuce instead of grated in the dressing.
- Of course, you can add a few strips of cooked bacon or pancetta, crumbled on top of the salad.

Thai Chicken Salad

If you have a pool, patio, or deck, this salad is the perfect menu starter. In fact, it is one of the many recipes I have that can be a meal on its own. Serve the chicken fresh off the grill and the salad will be warm, or choose to make it in advance and it works just as well. Since it has a rich-tasting dressing with no dairy, it is perfect for those watching their carbohydrates as well as their lactose intake.

Serves 4
as a main course

2	medium boneless, skinless chicken breasts	2
	Zest of 1 orange and 1 lime	
2	heads Boston lettuce, washed and torn	2
1	medium red pepper, chopped	1
1	medium red onion, sliced	1
1 cup	bean sprouts	250 mL
	Fresh coriander, chopped	
2	oranges, sectioned	2

Dressing

2	cloves garlic, finely chopped	2
1/3 cup	rice wine vinegar	75 mL
1/2 cup	roasted peanuts or peanut butter	125 mL
1	small dried chile, crushed (about 1 tsp/5 mL)	1
	Juice of 1 orange (about 1/2 cup/125 mL) and 1 lime	
1/4 cup	soy sauce	50 mL
1 tbsp	each sugar and sesame oil	15 mL

Rub chicken with orange and lime zest and grill over high heat for 4 minutes on each side, until cooked through. Cool and slice chicken into strips.

In a food processor, combine all ingredients for dressing and process until smooth.

Assemble salad by tossing lettuce, red pepper, red onion, sprouts, coriander, and chicken slices. Serve with a few orange segments and drizzle with dressing.

PREP

- The salad can also be made in winter, by grilling the chicken indoors, by cooking it over high heat in 15 mL (1 tbsp) sesame oil, or by searing it in a skillet and then roasting it for about 10 minutes, or until juices run clear.

OPTIONS

- If you are allergic to peanuts, try fresh cashews or 50 mL (1/4 cup) cashew butter or tahini (sesame paste).
- You can substitute shrimp or beef for the chicken for a different twist.

Fresh Tuna with Sprouts and Citrus Soy Dressing

Serves 4 to 6

This is an elegant Asian starter that not only looks incredible but combines the delicious flavours of ginger, lime, and honey with a clean, citrus hit of grapefruit. Again, I have chosen simple preparation and interesting ingredients to make your experience in the kitchen more enjoyable.

8 oz	fresh tuna	*227 g*
1	small head Boston lettuce, washed and torn	*1*
2	green onions, sliced	*2*
1 cup	bean sprouts	*250 mL*
1	carrot, coarsely grated	*1*
1	medium pink grapefruit, sectioned (optional)	*1*

Dressing

1/2 tsp	fresh ginger, finely chopped	*2 mL*
1/4 tsp	finely chopped fresh (or dried) chile	*1 mL*
	Juice of 1/2 lime and 1/2 lemon	
2 tbsp	each soy sauce and rice wine vinegar	*30 mL*
1 tsp	honey	*5 mL*
2 tsp	sesame oil	*10 mL*
1/2 tsp	dry mustard	*2 mL*
1/4 cup	peanut oil	*50 mL*

Combine all ingredients for dressing in food processor.

Rub tuna with 1/4 of dressing and cook over high heat on grill or in broiler for about 4 minutes on each side. Tuna should be pink in the middle. Set aside to cool. Slice thinly.

In medium bowl, combine lettuce, green onions, sprouts, and carrot. Toss with dressing.

Divide salad among 4 plates. Arrange tuna slices on top and drizzle with more dressing. Arrange grapefruit sections on top, if desired.

PREP

- Asking for sushi-grade tuna will ensure that you get fresh tuna, be it for sushi or for a salad like this one.
- It's best to grill the tuna steak whole, set it aside, and slice it immediately before serving.

OPTION

- For a low-fat version of the dressing, omit the lemon juice and peanut oil.

North African Salad with Toasted Ricotta

Serves 4 to 6

This salad is unusual because all of its ingredients are combined together without making a separate dressing, in typical North African style. Don't be alarmed by the name of this dish, because you're quite familiar with all its components. The only difference is that you've probably never prepared them this way before. All right, so you haven't toasted much ricotta lately, but you should give it a try. It's a great way to add flavour and texture to a simple salad.

2	medium field tomatoes, cut into 1-in/2.5-cm cubes	*2*
1	English cucumber, cut into 1-in/2.5-cm cubes	*1*
1/2	green pepper, cut into 1-in/2.5-cm cubes	*1/2*
1/2	red pepper, cut into 1-in/2.5-cm cubes	*1/2*
3	green onions, chopped	*3*
2	cloves garlic, minced	*2*
2 tbsp	red wine vinegar	*30 mL*
	Juice of 1 lime	
1/4 cup	each fresh mint and fresh parsley	*50 mL*
1/4 cup	extra virgin olive oil	*50 mL*
1/4 cup	each black olives and green olives	*50 mL*
	Salt and freshly cracked black pepper, to taste	
4 oz	pressed ricotta cheese	*114 g*

Combine all ingredients, except cheese, in a large bowl. Toss well to combine. Set aside.

Meanwhile, preheat oven to 180°C (350°F). Spread ricotta on baking sheet lined with parchment paper. Toast for 10 to 15 minutes, stirring frequently to get even colour. Remove and cool slightly.

Sprinkle cheese over salad before serving.

Vietnamese Vegetable Rolls

Makes 8 rolls

These fabulous rolls are perfect for a cocktail party or an informal gathering. They're a little tricky to get the hang of because the rice paper is difficult to work. Once you get it, though, you'll find them almost therapeutic to assemble. They're also perfect for vegetarians (see Options) or to give your palette a break from the heavier norm in appetizers.

1	medium carrot, julienned	*1*
1/2	small red pepper, julienned	*1/2*
2	green onions, cut into thin strips	*2*
1/2 cup	bean sprouts	*125 mL*
8	each lettuce leaves, whole leaves fresh mint, and whole leaves fresh coriander	*8*
5 oz	rice noodle vermicelli	*142 g*
8	medium rice paper sheets	*8*

Dipping sauce

1 tbsp	nuoc mam fish sauce, or any other Asian fish sauce	*15 mL*
1/4 cup	lime juice	*50 mL*
1	each small clove garlic and small chile, minced	*1*
1 tsp	honey	*5 mL*
1/2 tsp	grated ginger	*2 mL*
	Chopped peanuts (optional)	

Keep vegetables in separate piles, covered in moist paper towel, until ready to assemble rolls. Wash herb leaves thoroughly and set aside until ready to use. Boil noodles for 1 minute and immerse immediately in cold water. Drain.

Working with one rice paper sheet at a time, dip into a shallow pan containing about 1 cm (1/2 in) water. Remove quickly and set on counter to soften slightly. Do not use too much water or rolls will fall apart. Line rice paper with 1 lettuce leaf and then place small bunch of each vegetable side by side on middle of roll horizontally. Add a small bunch of noodles. Top with 1 leaf each of coriander and mint. Tuck sides of paper into centre and roll tightly like a cigar. Repeat with remaining rice papers.

Combine all ingredients for sauce in bowl and blend. Serve rolls cut in half diagonally with small bowl of sauce in middle of plate for dipping.

PREP

- When assembling the rolls, have all ingredients in front of you and work with one piece of rice paper at a time.
- Although the rolls can be stored in the fridge covered with moistened paper towels and plastic, they do not last for more than a few hours. It's best to chop all ingredients and make the sauce the day before. Assembly should take place the day you want to eat them.

OPTIONS

- Smoked duck, chicken, or shrimp can be added to give these rolls more character.
- To make sauce for vegetarians, omit the fish sauce.
- Vegetables of your choice can be substituted or added to rolls, but use ones that are crisp and can be eaten raw.

Navy Bean and Shell Pasta Soup with Pistou

In the Mediterranean, it's quite common to dine on a simple soup with plenty of fresh bread and olives. The beans give you added protein and you get even more for your efforts by adding pasta shells. Pistou is a French version of pesto, without the pine nuts and cheese.

Serves 6 to 8

2 tbsp	olive oil	*30 mL*
1	large onion, chopped	*1*
2	leeks, white part only, sliced	*2*
3	small cloves garlic, sliced	*3*
2	bay leaves	*2*
3	sprigs fresh thyme	*3*
2	stalks celery, sliced	*2*
2	medium carrots, cut in half lengthwise and sliced	*2*
8 cups	chicken stock (or vegetable stock)	*2 L*
1/2 cup	dried navy beans (soaked for 4-6 hours) or canned	*125 mL*
3/4 cup	small shell pasta (good quality)	*175 mL*
	Salt and freshly cracked black pepper, to taste	
	Parmesan cheese (optional)	

Pistou

1	large bunch basil, leaves only, washed and dried	*1*
1	small clove garlic, crushed	*1*
1/3 cup	extra virgin olive oil	*75 mL*

PREP
- If using canned beans, drain them and add with pasta. See the Mis en Place section for a quick-soak method for beans.

OPTIONS
- Using canned beans will save you soaking time, but you will lose a little bit of texture.
- Use chicken stock instead of vegetable stock for a more complex flavour.

In large pot, heat oil over high heat. Add onion and leek. Sweat for 3 to 4 minutes, or until soft. Add garlic, bay leaves, thyme, celery, and carrot and cook for 3 minutes, or until golden, stirring frequently. Add stock and beans (if using dried) and bring to a boil. Cover and reduce heat to low. Simmer until beans are tender but still have a bite to them, about 20 to 25 minutes. Add pasta, salt, and pepper. Cover again and increase heat to medium-high. Cook for 7 to 9 minutes, or until pasta is tender. Remove from heat.

Meanwhile, combine all ingredients for pistou in a food processor and pulse until smooth. To serve, spoon the soup into bowls, add a heaping dollop of pistou to each, and sprinkle with Parmesan cheese, if desired.

Vegetable Borscht with Cumin Sour Cream

Serves 6 to 8

Here's an unusual recipe for me, because it's actually very traditional. This hearty broth is great for cool weather and lends itself to many variations. I guess that's why I've created a recipe for it. You can make it a beef, chicken, or even a vegetable broth, and it can be served hot or cold. Personally, I don't like cold soups with meat bases, but it's up to you. Although the soup is quite hearty, it's actually quite low in fat if you don't serve it with sour cream.

2 tbsp	vegetable oil	*30 mL*
2	large onions, chopped	*2*
1/2	head green cabbage, finely chopped	*1/2*
2	stalks celery, chopped	*2*
1	large bunch beets, peeled, julienned or grated, or 1 16-oz/454-g can	*1*
1 tsp	caraway seeds	*5 mL*
1	bay leaf	*1*
4 cups	chicken stock	*1 L*
2 tbsp	red wine vinegar	*30 mL*
1/4 cup	brown sugar	*50 mL*
	Salt and freshly cracked black pepper, to taste	
1/4 cup	sour cream or yoghurt	*50 mL*
1 tsp	toasted cumin seeds, ground	*5 mL*
	Chopped chives (for garnish)	

In a large pot, over medium heat, sauté onions in oil until soft, about 3 minutes. Add cabbage, celery, beets, caraway seeds, and bay leaf. Cover with chicken stock; reduce heat to a simmer and cook for about 35 to 45 minutes until vegetables are tender.

Add vinegar and sugar and season with salt and pepper.

Combine sour cream with cumin and stir well.

Serve soup with a dollop of sour cream, if desired, and sprinkle with chives.

PREP

- Raw beets can be grated easily with the medium grating attachment on your food processor.
- Use latex or rubber gloves if you don't want to stain your hands with pink beet juice.
- This soup is ideal for freezing and for making the day before and storing in the fridge.
- If you are freezing the soup, don't add the sour cream until you are ready to serve.

OPTIONS

- This soup is a shoo-in for vegetarians; simply use vegetable stock instead of chicken.
- For a low-fat version, use non-fat yoghurt in the garnish instead of sour cream.
- If you want to go crazy on the purple, use red cabbage in place of the green.

Gazpacho

Serves 6 to 8

This is a classic soup recipe from Spain that is simply refreshing on a warm summer day. There are many options, as always, but you should always serve it ice cold and only in summer. It's a perfect starter for any grilled shrimp dish or try it with the Latin Rice and Peas with Chorizo and Mussels (see page 103). All the work is in the chopping, but the rest is a piece of cake.

4	large, vine-ripened or beefsteak tomatoes, peeled and chopped	*4*
2	stalks celery, diced	*2*
1	red pepper, diced	*1*
1	green pepper, diced	*1*
1	small sweet onion, diced	*1*
4	green onions, chopped	*4*
1/2	jalapeño chile, seeded and finely chopped	*1/2*
1	cucumber, peeled and chopped	*1*
2	cloves garlic, chopped	*2*
2 cups	stale bread, torn	*500 mL*
	Juice of 1 lime	
1/4 cup	vodka	*50 mL*
1/4 cup	olive oil	*50 mL*
	Salt and freshly cracked black pepper	
	Coriander, chopped	
1/2	bunch fresh parsley, leaves only, chopped	*1/2*

Save 1/4 each of cucumber, red pepper, green pepper, green onion, and celery for garnish.

Purée remaining vegetables with bread and lime juice in blender or pass through food grinder, working with 1/3 at a time.

Transfer to a bowl and stir in vodka and olive oil. Add salt and pepper to taste. Chill and serve with chopped herbs and remaining diced vegetables sprinkled over each bowl.

PREP

- All vegetables should be chopped before beginning the preparation of this soup.
- If you have a food grinder attachment on a mixer, use it to get the proper texture for this soup.
- Gazpacho should be served very cold, and is best served on the day it's prepared.

OPTIONS

- Remove the bread, olive oil, garlic, vodka and divide this recipe in half to make a great homemade vegetable juice.
- Substitute a yellow tomato, when available, for one of the red tomatoes to give this soup a beautiful bright-yellow hue and a touch more sugar.

Hot and Sour Soup
with Scallops

Serves 4 to 6

PREP

- Don't worry about the size of the scallops— simply adjust your cooking time according to their size. If using mammoth scallops, make sure you bring the soup back to a gentle simmer for a couple of minutes before adding the noodles.

- To make best use of your time, julienne the vegetables while the soup is simmering.

OPTIONS

- Replace scallops with boneless chicken legs, fish stock with chicken stock, and lime juice with lemon juice and you have a great variation on this delicious soup. You need to keep the chicken simmering in the broth to cook it through.

- Eliminate the scallops and you can serve this as a vegetarian broth before a rich main course.

- If you cannot find lemongrass, substitute the zest of 2 lemons.

This is a clean-tasting soup inspired by the spices of Thailand. It's my version of a hot and sour soup that you can create with ease in your own kitchen. The secret to mastering a lot of the mystical foods of Asia is learning about the ingredients. This recipe calls for fresh lemongrass; the only mystery is knowing where to buy it. I have become addicted to its unique lemon flavour.

1/2 tsp	sesame oil	*2 mL*
1 tbsp	vegetable oil	*15 mL*
1	small onion, chopped	*1*
1 tsp	grated fresh ginger	*5 mL*
1 lb	whole scallops (about 12 medium)	*454 g*
1	small Thai chile, chopped	*1*
6 cups	fish stock (chicken stock can be substituted)	*1.5 L*
	Juice of 1 lime	
3	stalks lemongrass, cut across white, tender end	*3*
4 oz	vermicelli rice noodles	*114 g*
	Salt and pepper, to taste	
1	small carrot, julienned or grated	*1*
1	green onion, thinly sliced	*1*
1/2	red pepper, julienned	*1/2*
	Several sprigs each of fresh mint and coriander, chopped	

Heat oils in a large pot on high. Add onion and sauté for several minutes. Add ginger and sauté for 1 or 2 minutes. Add scallops and sear for 1 minute on each side, until golden. Remove scallops and reserve.

Add chile, stock, and lime juice and bring mixture to a boil. Add lemongrass. Reduce heat to low and simmer, covered, for 30 minutes, or until lemon flavour is extracted from lemongrass. Remove lemongrass.

Add scallops back to soup. Sprinkle with vermicelli noodles and season with salt and pepper. Remove from heat and let stand 2 to 3 minutes, or until noodles are tender. Serve immediately.

To serve, divide sliced vegetables among soup bowls. Pour in soup and top with herbs.

Spicy Lentil Soup

Serves 4 to 6

Lentils are pulses. Introducing lentils into children's diets early will make it easier for them to acquire a taste for these pulses. Take advantage of this simple, nutritious soup that can be whipped together in no time. I have combined green and red lentils in this recipe. The red lentils will cook much faster, almost giving a creamy texture to the soup.

3 tbsp	olive oil	*45 mL*
1	large onion, chopped	*1*
4	cloves garlic, sliced lengthwise	*4*
1/2 tsp	cumin seed, chopped	*2 mL*
1/2 cup	green lentils	*125 mL*
1/2 cup	red lentils	*125 mL*
1	small dried chile, crushed	*1*
2	carrots, diced	*2*
2	stalks celery, diced	*2*
2	bay leaves	*2*
6 cups	vegetable stock	*1.5 L*
	Salt and pepper, to taste	
1 tbsp	red wine vinegar	*15 mL*

Sauté onions in olive oil on medium heat until golden. Add garlic and cumin seed and continue to cook for 2 to 3 minutes, or until garlic is golden.

Add all remaining ingredients, except vinegar, and bring to a boil. Cover and reduce heat to low. Simmer, covered, for 30 minutes.

Uncover and simmer for a further 10 to 15 minutes, or until lentils are tender. Adjust seasoning and add vinegar.

PREP

• This soups freezes well for several weeks and keeps in the fridge for several days.

OPTION

• Add 125 mL (1/2 cup) of rice, brown rice, or uncooked pasta to the soup for the final 10 to 12 minutes of simmering and make it almost like a stew.

Curried Sweet Potato and Apple Soup

Serves 4 to 6

This soup screams fall or winter. It's ideal for a festive gathering but can be prepared easily on any day of the week. I always use a good-quality, British, prepared curry powder.

1 tbsp	vegetable oil	*15 mL*
1	large cooking onion, chopped	*1*
1	medium carrot, chopped	*1*
2	large cloves garlic, chopped	*2*
2	stalks celery, chopped	*2*
1 tsp	chopped ginger	*5 mL*
1	leek, chopped (white part only)	*1*
3	medium sweet potatoes, peeled and chopped	*3*
1	medium apple, Granny Smith or other tart variety, peeled and chopped	*1*
5 cups	chicken stock	*1.25 L*
1/2 cup	dry white wine	*125 mL*
1 tsp	curry powder	*5 mL*
	Salt and pepper, to taste	

PREP
- Like most other puréed soups without dairy, this one is perfect for freezing.
- It also keeps for several days in the fridge and can be reheated easily.

OPTIONS
- If you want a chunkier soup, purée only half of the soup.
- Pears can be used instead of apples for a sweeter taste.
- Add 125 mL (1/2 cup) of cream at the end of cooking after soup is puréed to give it a smooth, creamy finish.

In a large pot over medium heat, sauté onions in oil for 2 minutes, or until soft. Add carrot, garlic, celery, ginger, and leek and sauté lightly, stirring with a wooden spoon until leeks are soft, about 3 to 4 minutes. Add remaining ingredients and stir. Bring to a boil.

Cover and reduce heat to low. Cook soup until potatoes are tender, about 25 minutes. Adjust seasoning.

Purée soup in a food processor and heat through.

Serve sprinkled with fresh chopped parsley as garnish.

Accompanying Your Dish

Baked Sweet Potato Batons

Serves 4

There's no reason to get bored of sweet potatoes. Cutting them a different way and tossing them in a few different spices can be quite fulfilling. These were originally made as an accompaniment to Grilled Chicken Wrapped in a Tortilla with Chipotle Sour Cream (see page 78). The chipotle mayonnaise is delicious on the potatoes. Remember that sweet potatoes are high in vitamins C and A and are not related to white potatoes, botanically speaking.

3	medium sweet potatoes, peeled, cut into 1/2 x 3-in sticks/1 x 7.5-cm	3
1 tbsp	melted butter *15 mL*	
1 tbsp	vegetable oil *15 mL*	
	Salt and freshly cracked black pepper, to taste	
Pinch	ground cloves *Pinch*	
Pinch	ground cinnamon *Pinch*	
1/4 tsp	cayenne *1 mL*	
	Juice of 1/2 lime (optional)	

Preheat oven to 190°C (375°F).

Combine all ingredients, except lime juice, in large bowl and toss well until combined.

Lay potatoes in single layer on large baking sheet lined with parchment paper.

Bake on lower rack of oven for 15 to 18 minutes, or until potatoes are golden, turning a few times.

Turn broiler on and cook for 3 minutes, or until potatoes begin to brown.

Remove from broiler and add lime juice, if desired.

PREP

- If you don't have a baking sheet large enough to cook all the potatoes at once, try baking them in two batches, so they don't steam.

- Once cooked, the potatoes will begin to lose their crisp texture, so they should be enjoyed right away; or you can eat them at room temperature but they may not be quite as crisp.

OPTION

- Use all vegetable oil (rather than butter and vegetable oil) if you are watching your cholesterol.

Low-Fat Stuffed Baked Potatoes

These spuds are a beautiful way to enjoy creamy potatoes without all the fat. (Of course, you can always use full-fat sour cream and regular cheese if you like.) They will be the perfect accompaniment to any grilled or roasted meat or fish. You can even make the whole thing in advance, stuff the potatoes, and keep them in the fridge until ready to bake. It doesn't get any easier than this.

Serves 4

2	baking potatoes	2
2 oz	low-fat Monterey Jack cheese, grated	57 g
1	small chile pepper, finely chopped	1
1/4 cup	chopped fresh parsley	50 mL
1/4 cup	chopped fresh chives	50 mL
1/3 cup	low-fat (1%) sour cream	75 mL
	Salt and freshly cracked black pepper, to taste	

Preheat oven to 180°C (350°F). Wash potatoes, pierce with fork several times, and bake for 40 to 45 minutes, or until tender. Cool until warm to the touch. Slice in half lengthwise.

Scoop contents of potatoes into medium bowl. Mash potatoes with food mill or masher. Combine with rest of ingredients and fill skins with potato mixture, mounding slightly. Place on a baking sheet lined with foil and bake for 15 to 20 minutes, or until golden and warmed through.

OPTIONS

- Add some fresh grilled salmon, flaked into the potato mixture, for a complete lunch course.
- Substitute blue cheese for the Monterey Jack and add some grilled onions, finely chopped, for a sharp alternative.

Variations on Mashed

Here are four variations on mashed potatoes that are completely different. Each one suits a different mood, purpose, or customer. I developed these because mashed potatoes are in demand, but they don't have to be predictable. You know how I hate being predictable!

yukon gold potato and st. andré phyllo blossoms

This is a simple preparation with an upscale presentation. The phyllo wrapped around the St. André–studded potatoes, gives them a crisp and mysterious shell. They can be served with any grilled or roasted meat, or even with fish. I would suggest you save them for special occasions, when you have a little more time.

5	medium Yukon Gold potatoes, peeled	5
3 oz	St. André cheese (or other soft, rich French cheese)	85 g
1 tbsp	chopped fresh chives	15 mL
1/3 cup	milk	75 mL
1 tbsp	butter	15 mL
	Salt and pepper, to taste	
4	sheets phyllo pastry	4
1-2 tbsp	vegetable oil	15-30 mL

Boil potatoes in salted water until tender. Drain and let cool slightly. Use a ricer or a food mill to mash potatoes. Add the cheese, chives, milk, butter, salt, and pepper. Stir well with a wooden spoon until potatoes are well combined.

Meanwhile, preheat oven to 180°C (350°F).

Cut phyllo sheets in half lengthwise, then crosswise, creating 16 rough squares. Brush with oil. Place 1 square on top of another and spoon 1/8 of potato mixture into centre. Loosely bunch phyllo into a bundle and place on baking sheet lined with parchment paper or brushed with oil. Repeat with remaining phyllo squares and potato mixture. Bake on middle rack of oven for 12 to 15 minutes, or until phyllo is golden and crispy.

Makes 8 bundles.

PREP

- Try to buy phyllo at a reputable grocer who probably goes through more stock; Greek or Middle Eastern stores are best. Always buy two, in case the first is dry.

- Never use a mixer or whisk to stir potatoes because it can make them gummy.

- Using a food mill, masher, or ricer is the best way to mash the potatoes.

OPTION

- You can use goat cheese instead of St. André cheese.

yukon gold roasted garlic mash

These mashed potatoes are the perfect blend of cream and buttermilk, with the addition of the roasted garlic that has become so popular these days. When you roast the garlic, its flavour changes from pungent to rich and sweet. This way you get all the benefits of garlic without having to kill everyone around the table with your breath. The rule is that when everyone is eating raw garlic, you're all in the same boat. I would stay away from it on a first date or if you're trying to get a big promotion.

1	head garlic, roasted	*1*
6	medium Yukon Gold potatoes, peeled and cut in half	*6*
2 tbsp	butter	*30 mL*
1/2 cup	buttermilk	*125 mL*
Pinch	freshly grated nutmeg	*Pinch*
	Salt and pepper, to taste	
1 tbsp	each fresh parsley and chives	*15 mL*

Preheat oven to 190°C (375°F).

To roast garlic, wrap head in foil paper and place in preheated oven. Roast for 35 to 40 minutes, or until garlic is soft. Remove from foil and squeeze out garlic. Set aside.

Meanwhile, in a medium pot, cover potatoes with cold water. Season with salt and cook on high until tender (about 30 minutes). Drain and mash in ricer or with a potato masher. Do not whisk or beat.

Return potatoes to pot. Add butter, milk, nutmeg, garlic, salt, and pepper. Stir over medium heat until light and fluffy. To finish, add freshly chopped herbs.

Serves 6.

no-butter mashed potatoes

This variation is perfect for anyone who is lactose intolerant or watching their cholesterol, or simply for anyone who ate way too many croissants for breakfast. Make sure you use a great-quality olive oil because it is going to take the place of butter and cream—and, as we know, those are big shoes to fill.

PREP

• In this variation, it is particularly important not to whisk the potatoes or they will go gummy. The lack of milk will turn them to glue much faster.

OPTIONS

• You can substitute any type of baking potato, such as russet.

• Add a couple more cloves of garlic and you have Greek skordalia, a dip for vegetables and fish cakes.

6	medium Yukon Gold potatoes, peeled and cut in half	6
1/4 cup	extra virgin olive oil	50 mL
1	clove garlic, minced	1
Pinch	freshly grated nutmeg	Pinch
2 tbsp	fresh parsley	30 mL
3	green onions, finely chopped	3
	Salt and freshly cracked black pepper, to taste	

In a medium pot, cover potatoes with cold water. Season with salt and cook on high until tender (about 30 minutes). Drain and mash in ricer or with potato masher. Do not whisk or beat.

Return potatoes to pot. Add olive oil, garlic, nutmeg, and pepper. Stir over very low heat until light and fluffy. Add parsley and green onion and stir to combine.

Serves 6.

yukon gold potato and pepper squash purée

Blending the potatoes with some squash gives the cook of the house the ability to fool his or her patrons. Squash is one of those orange vegetables that are so healthy but often not enjoyed. The final purée will have a beautiful peachy hue that will suit any occasion. It takes a little longer to prepare because of the squash.

1	medium pepper squash	*1*
	Brown sugar, to taste	
	Freshly grated nutmeg, to taste	
3	medium Yukon Gold potatoes	*3*
1 tsp	salt	*5 mL*
1/4 cup	butter	*50 mL*
1/3 cup	milk	*75 mL*
	Salt and pepper, to taste	

Preheat oven to 190°C (375°F).

Cut squash in quarters and remove seeds. Place skin side down on roasting pan. Dot with butter and sprinkle with brown sugar and nutmeg. Cover with foil and bake for 40 minutes, or until tender when tested with fork.

Meanwhile, cut potatoes into quarters and put in medium pot. Cover with cold water and add salt. Bring to a boil, then reduce to a simmer and boil gently, uncovered, until potatoes drop from fork when tested (about 20 to 30 minutes).

Scrape flesh of squash out with a large spoon and transfer to food mill. Strain potatoes and add to squash. Process the two in the food mill. Transfer to a saucepan and add butter, milk, and seasoning. Stir over medium heat until fluffy, about 4 minutes. Do not overmix.

Serves 6.

PREP

- Since this variation takes more time for the squash to cook, you can cook the squash in the microwave, covered with plastic wrap.

OPTION

- You can use cream instead of milk to give the potatoes a richer flavour.

Potato and Celery Root Gratin

Serves 8

"Potato gratin" is the official French way to say scalloped potatoes. By boiling the potatoes on the stovetop before baking them, they take about half the time. By the way, please don't pronounce it "grotten"; it should be "gra-ta." Try serving this with the Vanilla Bourbon Baked Ham (see page 131).

1-1/2 lb	Yukon Gold potatoes, peeled and thinly sliced (about 4 medium)	*681 g*
1	clove garlic, minced	*1*
1	piece celery root, peeled, cut in half, and sliced thinly	*1*
1 cup	cold milk (or enough to cover potatoes)	*250 mL*
1	sprig fresh rosemary	*1*
Pinch	nutmeg	*Pinch*
	Salt and pepper, to taste	
1 cup	10% cream	*250 mL*
1/4 cup	breadcrumbs (optional)	*50 mL*

Preheat oven to 200°C (400°F). Butter a medium baking dish (21 x 27.5 cm/8.5 x 11 in).

In a medium pot, cover potatoes, garlic, and celery root with milk and bring to a boil. Add rosemary and nutmeg, reduce heat to low, and simmer uncovered for 10 minutes, or until potatoes are almost tender.

Spread potato and celery root slices on bottom of baking dish and cover with cooking liquid. Season with salt and pepper. Pour enough cream over top to cover potatoes. Press potatoes and celery root down until completely immersed and sprinkle with breadcrumbs, if desired.

Bake until potatoes are tender and golden and top is crispy, about 20 minutes.

Let stand 10 minutes before serving.

PREP

- In my opinion, this is the simplest way to cook scalloped potatoes because the starch helps to give them a thick, creamy texture. Be sure to allow the dish to stand for the allotted time, as the potatoes will continue to absorb moisture.

OPTION

- See the other two potato gratin recipes (pages 45 and 46) that are variations of this one.

Yoghurt-Crusted Potato Gratin

This is yet another variation on potato gratin that I created for an Indian fusion cooking class. People loved it because the caraway and yoghurt gave the potatoes a nutty, tangy taste. It would be delicious served with spicy chicken or meat, as the yoghurt has a cooling effect on the palette.

Serves 6 to 8

2 lb	Yukon Gold potatoes, peeled and thinly sliced	*1 kg*
1-1/2 cups	milk	*375 mL*
3	sprigs fresh thyme	*3*
1 tbsp	butter	*15 mL*
1	large onion, thinly sliced	*1*
1	clove garlic, thinly sliced	*1*
1/2 tsp	caraway seeds	*2 mL*
	Salt and pepper, to taste	
1/2 cup	table cream (10%)	*125 mL*
3/4 cup	whole-fat yoghurt	*175 mL*

OPTION
• Eliminate the cream if you want a lighter version of the gratin.

Cover potatoes with milk in large pot and bring to a boil. Add thyme, reduce heat to low, and simmer, uncovered, for 10 minutes, or until potatoes are almost tender. Drain, reserving the liquid.

Meanwhile, preheat oven to 180°C (350°F). Butter a medium baking dish (at least 5-cm/2-in deep).

Sauté the onions, garlic, and caraway seeds in butter until soft. Season to taste.

Spread potato slices on bottom of baking dish. Sprinkle with onion mixture and salt and pepper. Repeat, layering potatoes and onions. Whisk together cream, yoghurt, and reserved cooking liquid. Pour over potatoes and press potatoes down firmly to completely cover.

Bake for 20 to 25 minutes, or until top of potatoes are golden and liquid has mostly evaporated. Remove and let stand for at least 10 minutes before serving.

Potato Gratin
with Herbes de Provence

Serves 6 to 8

PREP

- To make the preparation of this dish even easier, use the slicing attachment on your food processor to slice potatoes.

OPTION

- Herbes de Provence can be bought in the spice section of a specialty upscale grocer. Use a combination of thyme, rosemary, and marjoram as a substitute.

In this variation, the potatoes are cooked entirely in the oven. They will take longer, but you can work on something else in the meantime. This recipe has no dairy and relies only on the potatoes and herbs for flavour.

2 tbsp	extra virgin olive oil	*30 mL*
2 lb	Yukon Gold potatoes, peeled and thinly sliced	*1 kg*
2	cloves garlic, minced	*2*
1 tbsp	herbes de Provence	*15 mL*
	Salt and pepper, to taste	

Preheat oven to 180°C (350°F). Brush medium baking dish with half the oil. Spread 1/3 of potato slices on bottom of dish. Sprinkle with garlic, herbs, salt, and pepper. Repeat, layering potatoes in a circular pattern. Drizzle with remaining olive oil. Bake until potatoes are tender and top is golden, about 1-1/2 hours.

Pan-Fried Plantain

Serves 4

PREP

- Plantain is available at Asian or Caribbean markets, and is ripe when black and just starting to soften to the touch.

OPTION

- Plantain can be baked for a low-fat version, but it tends to be more starchy and dry when baked.

Plantain cannot be eaten raw like the common banana. Its skin will be black by the time its bright orange flesh ripens. If you buy it green, allow at least 10 days for it to ripen, or put it in a paper bag to hasten the process. This recipe is perfect with Jerked Swordfish Skewers with Red Lentils (see page 122).

1/4 cup	vegetable oil	*50 mL*
2	ripe plantain, peeled and cut into 1/8-in/3-mm slices	*2*
	Flour (for dredging)	

In large skillet, heat oil on high. Dredge plantain slices in flour very lightly. Fry for 2 minutes per side, or until golden. Transfer to tray lined with paper towel to drain oil. Serve with jerked swordfish or any Caribbean dish.

Vegetable Fried Rice

Serves 4 to 6

Fried rice is probably one of those things you only think about when ordering Chinese take-out. Once you see how easy it is to make, you may want to jazz it up your own way. That's what I do. It's the ideal way to use leftover rice and vegetables. The variations and possibilities are endless. This recipe is just my simple version, and I always say, "Don't be tied to recipes." For best results, make sure the rice is completely cooled before frying it.

1-3/4 cup	water	*425 mL*
1 cup	long-grain rice	*250 mL*
2 tbsp	vegetable oil	*30 mL*
1	small onion, chopped	*1*
1	clove garlic, chopped	*1*
1/2 tsp	chopped fresh ginger	*2 mL*
1	carrot, diced	*1*
1/2 cup	peas, fresh or frozen	*125 mL*
2	green onions, chopped	*2*
1	red pepper, chopped	*1*
5	medium mushrooms, sliced	*5*
1	dried chile pepper, crushed	*1*
1/4 cup	good-quality soy sauce	*50 mL*

In a medium saucepan, over high heat, bring water to a boil. Add rice, stir, and reduce heat to low. Cover and cook for 20 minutes without stirring. Remove from heat and let stand for 5 minutes. Remove rice from pan and spread on a baking sheet to cool completely. Transfer pan to fridge while chopping vegetables.

Heat oil on high in wok (for about 2 minutes). Add onion, garlic, ginger, and carrot and toss for 2 minutes. Add peas, green onions, red pepper, mushrooms, and chile and continue to toss over high heat for several minutes until vegetables are just soft. Add soy sauce and rice and toss until heated through (about 2 minutes).

PREP

- If making the rice fresh, the best way to use your time is to cook the rice first. Then, while it's cooking and cooling, you can organize the vegetables. Remember that the stir-frying takes a couple of minutes.

OPTIONS

- Add chicken, beef, or seafood to this dish and you have a full meal. Make sure you add the meat at the beginning of stir-frying so it is cooked through before adding the vegetables.

- You can substitute any of your favourite vegetables. Remember: Never become frustrated if you're missing an ingredient or two; improvise.

Wild Mushroom Risotto

Serves 8

- A restaurant trick that is sometimes used to improve timing is to half-cook the risotto and leave it very loose. Spread it out on a baking sheet and let it cool. Cover and set aside in fridge until you are ready to eat. Put it back in the pot and slowly begin to add more liquid over medium heat to achieve desired texture.

- The best rice for risotto is Carnaroli, but arborio super-fino will do just fine.

- The herbs, garlic, onions, and stock are a must because the rice absorbs and requires heavy flavour.

OPTIONS

- There are countless things you can add to risotto— shrimp, sausage, and peas, to name a few.

- You can use olive oil in place of the butter if you don't want animal fat, and you can also eliminate the pancetta. Use regular bacon if you can't find pancetta.

A well-made risotto seems to solve just about any problem. I still remember a white truffle risotto I had in New York that was creamy and studded with slivers of fresh white truffle. You don't have to be that extravagant, but adding wild mushrooms, fresh or dried, can give you a similar earthy flavour that seems to envelop the rice and impart its intensity. The secret to a perfect risotto is adding the liquid in small amounts so the rice will absorb it and create that creamy texture. It's not difficult to make, but it takes a little more muscle than a pilaf. It's perfect for entertaining because you can stir, chop, and talk with guests all at the same time.

2 cups	assorted wild mushrooms	*500 mL*
2 tbsp	butter	*30 mL*
2	large shallots, finely diced	*2*
2	large cloves garlic, chopped	*2*
1	sprig each fresh thyme and oregano	*1*
2	slices pancetta, diced (about 1 oz/28 g)	*2*
2 tbsp	olive oil	*30 mL*
1/2 cup	dry vermouth	*125 mL*
	Juice of 1/2 lemon	
	Zest of 1 lemon	
	Salt and freshly ground pepper	
2 cups	arborio super-fino rice	*500 mL*
6 cups	chicken stock, simmering	*1.5 L*
	Freshly grated Parmesan cheese, to taste (optional)	

Clean any dirt from mushrooms with paper towel. Rub well. Chop and set aside.

In a large, heavy pot, heat butter on high. Add shallots, garlic, thyme, oregano, and pancetta and sauté with wooden spoon until slightly soft (about 3 minutes). Add olive oil and mushrooms and continue to cook, stirring frequently. Reduce heat to medium and cook for 10 minutes, until mushrooms are completely soft. Add vermouth, lemon juice, and lemon zest, and season with salt and pepper. Add rice and continue to stir for about 3 minutes. Do not brown the rice.

Add 250 mL (1 cup) stock and stir. Reduce temperature to minimum. Simmer until liquid has evaporated. Continue this process until all stock has been used and rice is tender. Stir frequently. The whole process should take about 25 minutes.

Adjust seasoning and add Parmesan cheese, if desired.

Jasmine Rice

Serves 4

It's great to have a simple rice with a little personality to fall back on. This jasmine rice is fragrant and is what you get when you order steamed rice at a Thai restaurant. It's a great canvas for spicy curries, flavourful stews, and Asian stir-fries. Typically, jasmine rice is made without salt or any other seasoning. Since I'm in a traditional mood, this recipe will follow suit.

PREP

- Steaming is the best way to cook rice, as it absorbs moisture evenly and cooks better. If you have a steamer, use it and follow the manufacturer's instructions.

    1 cup   jasmine rice *250 mL*
1-3/4 cups water *425 mL*

Rinse rice under cool water to wash off some of the starch. Transfer to medium pot. Add water and bring rice to a boil over high heat. Reduce heat to low, cover, and simmer for 20 minutes. Remove from heat and set aside for 5 minutes without lifting cover.

Fluff with fork and serve with favourite main course.

Jamaican-Spiced Basmati Rice with Toasted Coconut

Serves 6

This recipe is my personal variation on Jamaican rice and peas. Traditionally, this dish is a combination of creamy coconut milk, gungo peas, and plenty of thyme and garlic. I'm creating a bit of Indian fusion by using basmati rice and adding cumin and coriander. Serve this any time you want a break from ordinary rice.

1/2 cup	dried red beans, soaked for about 4 hours (or 1 small can)	*125 mL*
	Salt and pepper, to taste	
2 tbsp	olive oil	*30 mL*
1/2 tsp	crushed toasted cumin	*2 mL*
1/4 tsp	crushed toasted coriander seeds	*1 mL*
1/8 tsp	ground allspice	*0.5 mL*
1/2 tsp	chopped fresh thyme	*2 mL*
1/2	chile pepper, chopped	*1/2*
1	small cooking onion, finely chopped	*1*
1	clove garlic, finely chopped	*1*
1-1/2 cups	basmati rice	*375 mL*
2	bay leaves	*2*
1/2 cup	coconut milk	*125 mL*
2 cups	chicken stock or water	*500 mL*
	Unsweetened coconut shards (available at health stores)	
	Fresh thyme	

PREP

- Consult Mise en Place for a quick-soak method for beans. If using canned beans, you will lose some texture but will save a lot of time.

OPTIONS

- Coconut milk is very common in the Caribbean, but you can certainly replace it with stock.
- Replace chicken stock with water or vegetable stock for a vegetarian option.

Drain beans and cover with cold water. Bring to a boil and simmer for 40 to 45 minutes, or until tender. Season with salt and pepper. Drain and set aside.

Meanwhile, in a medium pot, heat olive oil on high. Add spices and chile pepper and sauté for several minutes. Add onion and garlic and sauté for 3 to 4 minutes, or until soft and golden. Add rice and bay leaves and toss for 2 minutes until rice is completely coated in oil. Add coconut milk, stock or water, salt, and pepper. Bring to a boil and reduce heat to low. Cover and simmer for 14 minutes. Do not remove lid. Remove from heat and let stand for at least 5 minutes. Just before serving, toss in cooked beans and garnish with coconut shards and fresh thyme.

Roasted Shallot and Lemon Barley

Here's a delicious alternative to rice or pasta that only takes 35 minutes to cook and is worth the short wait. Using pearl barley gives you the taste of barley without the long cooking time. However, you do lose the outer bran layer, which contains a lot of the nutrients, but nothing comes without a cost. If you want to use pot barley, it needs to be soaked overnight. The addition of the roasted shallots and lemon make this dish flavourful enough to be a stuffing or simply a side dish.

Serves 4 to 6

4	large shallots, roasted whole	*4*
1 tbsp	olive oil	*15 mL*
2 tbsp	butter	*30 mL*
1	clove garlic, chopped	*1*
1 cup	pearl barley	*250 mL*
2	sprigs fresh thyme	*2*
	Zest of 1 lemon	
3 cups	chicken stock	*750 mL*
	Salt and pepper, to taste	

Preheat oven to 190°C (375°F). Peel shallots and toss in small roasting pan with olive oil. Roast until just soft and golden, about 20 minutes. Remove and cool slightly. Chop coarsely.

Combine butter and garlic in medium pot over medium heat. Sauté for 2 to 3 minutes, or until soft. Add shallots, barley, thyme, and lemon zest and cook for 1 minute.

Add stock and season. Bring to a boil and stir. Cover and simmer on low heat for 35 minutes, or until tender. Remove from heat and fluff with fork.

PREP
- Roasting the shallots gives the barley more flavour, but if you're in a hurry, you can simply chop and then gently sauté them to release some of the sugars.
- The barley will keep for a couple of days in the fridge and can be reheated easily in the microwave.

OPTION
- This recipe is easily transformed to vegetarian by substituting vegetable stock for the chicken stock.

Green Mango Salad

Serves 4 to 6

I made this salad on the show, but didn't give you the exact recipe; so I'm making sure you get it now. This is similar to but not exactly what you would get at a Thai restaurant, and it makes a fabulous tangy side dish to any stir-fry.

2	green mangoes, peeled and thinly sliced	2
1	red onion, thinly sliced	1
1	small clove garlic, minced	1
1	small Thai chile, minced	1
1 tbsp	vegetable oil	15 mL
1 tbsp	rice wine vinegar	15 mL
	Juice of 1/2 lime	
2 tbsp	sugar	30 mL
1 tsp	fish sauce	5 mL
3 tbsp	chopped fresh mint	45 mL
1 tbsp	chopped fresh coriander	15 mL
1/4 cup	chopped unsalted roasted peanuts	50 mL

Use a vegetable peeler to peel mango. Continue to use vegetable peeler to slice thin pieces of mango flesh until you get to the stone. Work your way evenly around all sides of mango. Alternately, you can use a mandolin, if you are adept. Combine mango and remaining ingredients in medium bowl and toss until well blended.

PREP

- Green mangoes are actually a variety found at Asian markets. They are not unripe mangoes.
- In Thai, fish sauce is called Nam Pla; it can be found at Asian stores.
- If you want to make this salad in advance, leave the peanuts out and sprinkle them on just before serving. The salad will keep for a couple of hours, but not much longer.

OPTIONS

- If you can't find fish sauce or choose to omit it, add a pinch of salt.
- Reduce or eliminate the Thai chile if you don't like the heat.

White Bean Salad
with Herbs and Swiss Chard

Although you could call this dish a salad, I would serve it as an accompanying dish rather than as a starter. So, I thought you'd make better use of it in the side dishes section. The tangy combination of lemon, garlic, and parsley is just the thing to spruce up the beans. At the end, I added some blanched Swiss chard, making it practically a meal on its own served alongside a grilled piece of fish. It also lends itself to being made in advance, as it gets better with age. Don't we all?

Serves 6 to 8

2	cloves garlic, minced	2
1	bunch Italian parsley, chopped	1
	Zest of 2 lemons	
	Juice of 1 lemon	
2 cups	cooked white beans	500 mL
3 tbsp	extra virgin olive oil	45 mL
	Salt and freshly cracked black pepper, to taste	
1	bunch Swiss chard, trimmed and sliced	1

OPTION
- Use rapini, dandelion greens, or beet greens instead of Swiss chard.

Combine all ingredients, except Swiss chard, in medium bowl and toss to combine. If using dried beans instead of canned, they must be soaked for about 4 hours, then cooked for about 25 minutes, or until tender.

Salad can be made in advance and stored, covered, in fridge. Just before serving, cook Swiss chard in rolling boiling salted water for 2 minutes, or until tender. Drain and cool. Add to salad and stir to combine. Adjust seasoning.

Spanakopita—Spinach Triangles

Yields about 15 triangles

Spanakopita is pronounced with the emphasis on the "ko." They are fairly easy to make once you get the hang of working with phyllo. This is another rare occasion when I am giving you a classical recipe, but you can fill these babies with just about anything under the sun. At my family gatherings, they are so popular that they are simply known as "triangles."

1 cup	fresh spinach, leaves only, chopped	*250 mL*
1 tsp	olive oil	*5 mL*
2	green onions, chopped	*2*
1 tbsp	chopped fresh dill	*15 mL*
2 oz	feta cheese, crumbled	*57 g*
2	eggs, beaten	*2*
	Salt and freshly cracked black pepper, to taste	
6	sheets phyllo pastry	*6*
1/4 cup	melted butter	*50 mL*

PREP
- You can substitute frozen spinach and simply thaw instead of boiling. If using fresh spinach, make sure to wash it thoroughly, as it traps a lot of sand and dirt.

- Triangles can be prepared and frozen before baking for those drop-in guests. Make sure you seal them in a plastic container to avoid freezer burn.

OPTION
- Melted butter can be replaced with olive oil if you are watching your saturated fats.

Preheat oven to 190°C (375°F).

Wash spinach and immerse in boiling salted water for about 3 minutes. Drain and rinse in cold water. Squeeze out excess moisture and reserve.

Heat oil in saucepan, add onion, spinach, and dill, and toss on high for 3 minutes, until onions soften. Remove and cool.

Combine cooled spinach mixture with feta, eggs, salt, and pepper. Set aside.

Cut each sheet of phyllo into 5 equal strips. Work with 1 pile of phyllo at a time. Wrap remaining phyllo in tea towel. Brush a strip with melted butter, cover with a second strip, and butter again. Lay strip down vertically in front of you. Spoon a heaping teaspoon of filling in bottom corner of strip and fold in half diagonally, creating a triangle. Continue folding over into triangular shape until you reach end of strip. Repeat with remaining strips. Brush tops with a little more butter. Place triangles on baking sheet and bake on middle rack of oven for about 15 minutes, or until golden.

Serve warm as appetizer or with your main course.

Don't Forget Your Veggies

Asian Vegetable Stir-Fry
with Crispy Bean Threads

Serves 4 to 6

This vegetarian stir-fry is colourful, delicious, and loaded with vitamins. It's the ideal dinner for the teenagers in the household who are trying to expand their vegetable knowledge. Try not to get bogged down with specific vegetables—use what you can find or what you have. The crispy bean threads add interesting new texture but can easily be replaced with noodles or rice.

1 cup + 2 tbsp	vegetable oil	*280 mL*
1/3	package (1-1/2 oz/42 g) bean threads	*1/3*
1	large onion, sliced	*1*
1	clove garlic, chopped	*1*
1 tsp	grated fresh ginger	*5 mL*
1	head broccoli, cut into florets	*1*
1	bunch bok choy, trimmed and sliced	*1*
6	shiitake mushrooms, sliced	*6*
3	stems mustard greens, trimmed and sliced	*3*
1/4 cup	good-quality soy sauce	*50 mL*
1 tbsp	hoisin sauce	*15 mL*
1/2 tsp	chile flakes	*2 mL*
2	carrots, sliced with vegetable peeler into very thin, long strips	*2*
1/2 cup	toasted, salted cashews	*125 mL*

PREP

- The secret to this or any stir-fry is to chop and slice the ingredients before you begin cooking.

- This recipe is perfect for households where people arrive at different times. When all the ingredients are chopped and the rice or noodles are cooked, the stir-fry can be whipped together in 3 to 5 minutes.

OPTION

- If you'd like to add beef or chicken, simply slice it thinly and stir-fry it briefly with the ginger. Remove it, continue the recipe, and add it back at the end so it doesn't dry out.

Heat 250 mL (1 cup) oil in medium skillet or wok on high. When oil appears hot, break a small piece of bean thread and toss gently into oil. If bean thread puffs, oil is hot enough. Break bean threads up into 3 small, flat piles. Toss quickly into oil, one at a time, and turn over rapidly only until puffed, about 30 seconds. Repeat with remaining threads. Remove from heat and drain on baking sheet lined with paper towels. Reserve for later.

In large wok or skillet, heat 30 mL (2 tbsp) of vegetable oil on high. Stir-fry onion for 2 minutes, or until soft. Add garlic, ginger, broccoli, bok choy, mushrooms, and mustard greens. Stir-fry for 2 to 3 minutes, or until greens have wilted and broccoli has begun to soften. Add soy sauce, hoisin, chile flakes, and carrots and cover for 1 minute, or until vegetables are done to your liking. Remove from heat and sprinkle with cashews.

Divide puffed bean threads among 4 plates and top with warm stir-fry.

Stir-Fried Bok Choy with Yellow Peppers

This quick stir-fry can be adapted to suit any purpose. Add chicken or beef, serve it over rice, and it's a meal in minutes. Bok choy is another versatile, crisp, mild Asian green that is readily available year-round in Asian markets.

1 tbsp	vegetable oil	*15 mL*
1 tbsp	chopped fresh ginger	*15 mL*
1	clove garlic, chopped	*1*
1	large bunch bok choy, washed, thick bottoms trimmed, and sliced	*1*
1	yellow pepper, diced	*1*
1/4 tsp	chile flakes	*1 mL*
2 tbsp	good-quality soy sauce	*30 mL*
1 tsp	black sesame seeds	*5 mL*

In wok or large skillet, heat oil on high. Add ginger and garlic and stir-fry for 1 to 2 minutes, or until just soft. Add remaining ingredients, except sesame seeds, and stir-fry for 3 to 4 minutes, or until bok choy is just soft.

Remove from heat and sprinkle with sesame seeds.

Serve with rice and any favourite meat or poultry.

PREP
- There is so little preparation for this recipe that you can just whip it together while your meat or other dishes are cooking
- Be sure to remove any rusty or discoloured leaves from bok choy, and wash the bottoms well, as they trap lots of dirt.

OPTION
- Try using baby bok choy, which is more tender and a lighter green colour.

Diana's Favourite
Autumn Vegetable Stir-Fry

Serves 4 to 6

This stir-fry is a combination of flavours from Asia and North America. The squash and maple syrup give you more substance, as well as a touch of sweetness. This recipe provides an innovative way to use all that squash in the fall. It's my cousin's favourite.

1	small butternut squash, peeled	1
1 tbsp	vegetable oil	15 mL
1 tsp	chile oil	5 mL
1	onion, cut into 1-in/2.5-cm squares	1
1	1/2-in/1-cm piece ginger, finely sliced and julienned	1
1	red pepper, cut into 1-in/2.5-cm squares	1
2 tbsp	water	30 mL
1/4 cup	soy sauce	50 mL
2 tbsp	maple syrup	30 mL
2	bunches bok choy (about 6 cups/1.5 L chopped)	2
Pinch	ground allspice	Pinch
	Salt and freshly ground pepper, to taste	

PREP

• If you want to buy prepackaged squash that is already peeled, simply make sure you slice it thinly before blanching to reduce your cooking time.

OPTIONS

• If you don't have chile oil, you can use 1/2 tsp (2 mL) chopped fresh chile or chile flakes.

• If you like the flavours but not the spice, omit the chile altogether.

Cut squash in half, lengthwise, and remove seeds. Cut into 3-mm (1/8-in) slices. Transfer to medium pot and cover with water. Bring to a boil and reduce to simmer for 2 minutes, or until just tender. Drain and reserve.

Meanwhile, in large wok or skillet, heat both oils on high and add onion and ginger. Sauté for 2 minutes, or until soft. Add red pepper and squash. Combine water, soy sauce, and maple syrup and pour over vegetables. Cover and steam on high for 1 minute. Remove lid and add bok choy. Toss gently and cover for 2 minutes, or until greens are just wilted. Adjust seasoning and serve.

Grilled Corn and Red Pepper Sauté

I developed this sweet combination of grilled corn and red peppers specifically to go with Grilled Lobster with Lemongrass Chive Butter (see page 105). Once you see and taste the two together, you will know that they are made for one another. But that's not to say that you can't serve it with any other summer fare.

Serves 4

2	ears fresh corn, husks removed	*2*
1 tbsp	butter	*15 mL*
1	red pepper, diced	*1*
	Salt and freshly cracked black pepper, to taste	
1 tbsp	fresh chives	*15 mL*

Preheat grill or barbecue.

Grill corn for 3 to 4 minutes, or until lightly charred, turning frequently.

Stand corn on cutting board, holding with one hand and placing flat end down to secure. Run knife along each side, rotating ear to remove kernels. Discard cob or save for stock.

Heat butter in large skillet over medium heat. Add pepper and corn and sauté for 3 to 4 minutes, or until peppers are soft and corn is tender. If corn still seems too firm, cover skillet and steam corn for 1 minute.

Remove from heat, season with salt and pepper, and add chives.

PREP

- If you're not quite comfortable removing the kernels from fresh corn, you can always use frozen corn and wrap it in foil. Pierce foil several times with a fork to get a little of the smoky flavour and grill for several minutes.

- You can grill the corn in advance, or even the day before, and sauté with the red peppers just before serving.

Lemon Rosemary Green Beans

Serves 4 to 6

I often add a little something to very simple recipes, thereby transforming them into something special with little or no extra work. Just by browning the butter slightly and adding a whole sprig of rosemary still intact, you get a nutty flavour that gives green beans quite a makeover.

1 lb	green beans, trimmed only at stem	*454 g*
1 tbsp	butter	*15 mL*
1	sprig rosemary, whole	*1*
	Zest of 1 lemon	
	Freshly cracked black pepper, to taste	

Blanch beans in salted boiling water for 2 minutes, or until just green and still crisp. Drain and reserve.

Meanwhile, heat butter in large skillet on high. Add rosemary and continue to heat until butter turns amber, about 30 seconds. Add lemon zest, pepper, and beans and toss for several seconds until beans are coated.

Remove rosemary sprig or use for garnish.

Serve with any of your favourite main dishes. My selection would be Salmon with Light White Wine Sabayon (see page 117).

PREP

- The green beans can be blanched ahead of time and heated through just before serving. This helps prevent overcooking them and losing their crunchy texture.
- Look in the glossary under "beurre noisette." That will explain the change in the butter.

OPTIONS

- Use thyme for a more delicate flavour, or parsley for even less intensity.
- Removing the rosemary leaves from the sprig and chopping them will give you the maximum intensity.

Rapini with Pine Nuts and Red Peppers

You can never have enough vegetables in your repertoire. It makes your life easier and keeps dinner interesting. You can introduce rapini by disguising it as broccoli, to which it is related. (It's also known as broccoli rabe.) Sometimes we have to be a little devious in order to make it work in the kitchen. In this recipe, the addition of red peppers and pine nuts softens its slightly bitter edge. Rapini makes my top three list of veggies.

Serves 4

1	bunch rapini, washed, thick stems trimmed about 2 in/5 cm from bottom	*1*
1/4 cup	pine nuts	*50 mL*
1	red pepper, diced	*1*
2 tbsp	extra virgin olive oil	*30 mL*
	Juice of 1/2 lemon (optional)	
	Freshly cracked black pepper, to taste	

Boil rapini in plenty of boiling salted water for 5 to 6 minutes, or until just tender but still firm. Drain and transfer to serving bowl.

Toast pine nuts in small, dry frying pan over moderate heat for several minutes, or until golden.

Sprinkle pine nuts and red pepper over rapini and drizzle with olive oil and lemon juice, if desired. Season with pepper.

PREP

- Avoid stir-frying or braising rapini, unless you really like its bitter taste. When blanched, as in this recipe, its bitter edge is reduced.
- The lemon juice helps to balance the flavour.

Moroccan Vegetable Tagine over Minted Couscous

Serves 6

North African spices have long been a favourite of mine. In this soothing tagine (stew), the vegetables take on a different complexion with the addition of the spices and olives. As always, you can use this as a guide and add the spices you have or can find. There's nothing worse than defeating yourself before you've even started the recipe. Adding the chickpeas provides perfect protein for vegetarians.

1	large onion, chopped	*1*
3	cloves garlic, chopped	*3*
3 tbsp	olive oil	*45 mL*
1	red pepper, diced	*1*
2	stalks celery, diced	*2*
2	carrots, diced	*2*
4	plum tomatoes (fresh or canned), diced	*4*
	Zest of 2 lemons, grated	
2 tsp	cumin seed, ground	*10 mL*
1/2 tsp	coriander seed, ground	*2 mL*
1/4 tsp	caraway seeds, ground	*1 mL*
1	stick cinnamon	*1*
1/4 tsp	each turmeric and sumac	*1 mL*
1	dried red chile, crushed	*1*
2 cups	vegetable stock or water	*500 mL*
1/4 cup	good-quality green olives, pitted	*50 mL*
1	can (19 oz/540 g) chickpeas	*1*
	Salt and pepper, to taste	

Sauté onion with garlic and olive oil in medium pot until onion is golden, about 3 to 5 minutes. Add red pepper, celery, carrots, tomatoes, and spices and cook 15 minutes on low heat. Add stock or water and olives. Cover and simmer without stirring for 10 to 15 minutes, or until carrots are just tender. Add chickpeas and cook 3 to 4 minutes just to get some flavour. Adjust seasoning.

PREP

- Don't spend a lot of time chopping the vegetables. Simply make sure the pieces are roughly the same size so they cook at the same time.

- This stew keeps beautifully, covered in the fridge for a few days or in the freezer for a few weeks.

- Sumac can be found at Middle Eastern stores or spice markets.

OPTION

- To simplify the preparation, buy a good-quality British-style curry powder and eliminate the spices, except for the cinnamon stick.

Minted Couscous

1 tbsp	olive oil	*15 mL*
1-3/4 cups	water	*425 mL*
	Salt and pepper, to taste	
1 cup	couscous (instant)	*250 mL*
1/4 cup	chopped fresh mint	*50 mL*

In medium saucepan, combine oil, water, salt, and pepper. Cover and bring to a boil. Remove from heat, stir in couscous, and cover immediately. Let stand for 5 minutes. Stir in mint and fluff with fork. Serve with tagine.

Dandelion Greens with Olive Oil and Lemon

Serves 4 to 6

I know you're thinking, "I pay to get rid of those weeds; I didn't know you could eat them." Europeans have been enjoying fresh dandelions for many years, but they are not exactly the ones that grow on your lawn. Most of them are cultivated and are not as bitter. They're simple to cook and high in calcium, iron, and vitamin A. Give them a try and you'll be surprised. They are delicious with fish.

1	large bunch dandelion greens, washed thoroughly	*1*
1/4 cup	extra virgin olive oil	*50 mL*
	Juice of 1 lemon	

Trim stems from greens about 7.5 cm (3 in) from bottom and discard.

Boil in plenty of boiling salted water in a deep pot. Cook until just tender, about 4 to 5 minutes. Drain and cool slightly.

Drizzle with olive oil and lemon juice.

PREP

- These greens are better served at room temperature or cold. They can be cooked, cooled, and covered in the fridge for several days. Add the lemon juice just before serving.

- Take special care in washing the greens, as they trap a lot of dirt.

Potato, Leek, and Rocquefort Strudel

Serves 6 to 8

This is definitely a meal on its own, but it can certainly accompany any hearty meat. The use of phyllo instead of traditional strudel dough simplifies the process and gives you the chance to make something very elegant with incredible flavour, without too much effort. It's a show-stopper for brunch.

2	medium Yukon Gold potatoes, peeled and cut into 1/8-in/3-mm slices	2
1	large onion, sliced	1
3	leeks, light part only, washed thoroughly and finely sliced	3
2	sprigs fresh thyme, chopped	2
1 tbsp	butter	15 mL
1/4 cup	chopped fresh chives	50 mL
2	sprigs fresh tarragon, chopped	2
2 tbsp	sour cream	30 mL
1 tbsp	lemon juice	15 mL
	Salt and freshly cracked black pepper, to taste	
4 oz	Rocquefort or other blue cheese, crumbled	114 g
5	sheets phyllo pastry	5
2-3 tbsp	olive oil (for brushing phyllo)	30-45 mL
1	egg white	1

Sauce

1 tsp	butter	5 mL
1/2	bulb fennel, finely sliced	1/2
1/2 cup	tomato sauce	125 mL
	Salt and pepper, to taste	
2 tbsp	cream (optional)	30 mL

Preheat oven to 190°C (375°F).

Immerse potatoes in cold water and cook in medium pot on high heat. Bring water to a boil, add salt, and reduce heat to medium. Cook uncovered until potatoes are tender, about 8 to 10 minutes. Drain and set aside.

Meanwhile, sauté onion with leeks and thyme in butter on medium-high heat until golden and caramelized, stirring frequently. Process should take about 20 minutes. Remove from heat and add chives, tarragon, sour cream, and lemon juice. Combine leek mixture with potatoes while both are still warm. Break potatoes up gently with a wooden spoon. Cool mixture and season with salt and pepper. Add cheese and blend, leaving chunks of cheese intact.

Line a baking sheet with parchment paper and brush 1 sheet of phyllo with olive oil. Turn phyllo with long side horizontally in front of you. Lay remaining phyllo sheets on top of first, one at a time, brushing each sheet with oil. Lay potato mixture along bottom edge of phyllo horizontally, leaving about 3.5 cm (1-1/2 in) on either side to tuck in strudel. Brush strudel with egg white along all edges to create a seal when baking. Begin rolling strudel like a jelly roll away from you. After first turn, tuck edges in and continue to roll. Brush strudel with olive oil and make 3 slits in the top.

Bake in oven for 20 to 25 minutes, or until golden and flaky. Remove and let stand 5 minutes. Slice while still warm.

Meanwhile, prepare sauce by sweating fennel in butter for 3 to 5 minutes, or until soft. Add tomato sauce. Simmer, covered, for 10 minutes until fennel is very tender. Season with salt and pepper. Add cream, if desired, and serve warm with strudel.

PREP

- The method seems to be involved, but actually it's quite simple. If you serve this with a simple salad, it stands as a full meal that gives you a break from meat.

- The potatoes can be boiled and the onion and leek mixture can be made several hours ahead, to save you some time.

OPTIONS

- Substitute any kind of blue cheese for Roquefort.

- For the lactose intolerant, omit the sour cream, blue cheese, and cream and change the butter to olive oil.

Snap Pea, Brussels Sprout, and Orange Pepper Sauté

Serves 4 to 6

I made this vegetable for a great client of mine who wanted an interesting small dinner party catered. The colour is absolutely beautiful and it's a great new way to use Brussels sprouts. There is no complication in this dish, which is why I always say, "Less is more."

1 cup	Brussels sprouts, trimmed and cut in half	*250 mL*
1 cup	snap peas, trimmed	*250 mL*
1 tbsp	butter	*15 mL*
1	orange pepper, cut into strips	*1*
	Salt and pepper, to taste	

Bring a medium pot of salted water to boil. Add Brussels sprouts and boil on high for 7 minutes, or until tender. With a slotted spoon, remove sprouts, return pot to heat, and when water boils, add snap peas. Cook for 3 minutes and strain.

Heat butter in skillet on high and add orange pepper. Sauté for 2 to 3 minutes, then add peas and sprouts and toss lightly just until shiny, about 1 minute. Season with salt and pepper and serve with favourite meat or fish.

PREP

• Vegetables can be chopped and Brussels sprouts can be blanched and set aside until ready to serve. This will allow you time to cook your main dish. The sauté will take about 3 minutes.

OPTION

• Snap peas are not always available, so use snow peas instead.

Winter Vegetable Roast

Serves 6

If you're looking for a way to enjoy the bounty of winter, here's a simple roasted vegetable concoction that could become a family favourite. It's so versatile, you could easily feature it for Thanksgiving or Christmas, or just make it in a snap on a weeknight.

2	medium heads celery root	2
2	medium sweet potatoes	2
16	medium Brussels sprouts, trimmed	16
1 tsp	freshly chopped sage	5 mL
1	sprig fresh thyme	1
Pinch	ground allspice	Pinch
1-1/2 tbsp	vegetable oil	22 mL
	Salt and pepper, to taste	

Preheat oven to 190°C (375°F).

Peel celery root and cut lengthwise into quarters, then in half, horizontally.

Peel potatoes and cut into 8 equal pieces each.

Combine all ingredients in a large bowl and toss several times until vegetables are well coated with oil and herbs. Season with salt and pepper. Transfer to a roasting pan and arrange so vegetables are not overlapping.

Roast on lower rack of oven for 30 to 35 minutes, turning often, until vegetables are tender but still slightly firm.

PREP
- Celery root is also know as celeriac, and is abundant from fall to winter.

OPTION
- If you add a little apple cider vinegar, you can serve this at room temperature as a hearty winter salad.

Stuffed Baby Eggplant

Serves 4 to 6

These baby eggplants are a staple in Greece. They always remind me of growing up, as my father used to make them quite often. This is one of my favourite ways to cook eggplant because the peppery skin intensifies and is balanced by the sweet combination of onion and garlic.

4	baby eggplants	4
1 tbsp	olive oil	15 mL
	Salt and pepper, to taste	

Stuffing

1 tbsp	olive oil	15 mL
2	cloves garlic, chopped	2
2	medium onions, diced	2
3	small plum tomatoes, peeled and diced	3
2 tbsp	assorted fresh herbs (basil, oregano)	30 mL
	Salt and pepper, to taste	
1/4 cup	Parmesan cheese (optional)	50 mL
3 oz	goat cheese (optional)	85 g

PREP

- Large eggplants would not be suitable for this dish, because they have too many seeds and are a little too bitter.

- These can be stored in the fridge for a couple of days and reheat well. If you leave out the cheese, they can also be frozen and sprinkled with cheese before serving.

- When cooking the onion and garlic, make sure to keep stirring them to prevent burning. You want a golden, sweet flavour from the onions.

OPTION

- You can also use Japanese eggplant— the thin, long, purple ones.

Preheat oven to 190°C (375°F).

Cut eggplant in half lengthwise and drizzle with olive oil. Season with salt and pepper. Bake on roasting pan or cookie sheet for about 20 minutes.

Remove from oven and scoop out the insides and keep for stuffing. Arrange eggplant in roasting pan lined with foil. Set aside.

Meanwhile, to prepare stuffing, combine oil, garlic, and onion in medium saucepan and sauté over moderate heat until soft and golden, about 5 to 7 minutes.

Add tomatoes, fresh herbs, salt, and pepper and cook for 5 minutes. Add reserved eggplant filling and check seasoning.

Fill eggplant shells with stuffing and sprinkle with cheese combination, if desired. Return to oven until golden on top, about 12 to 15 minutes.

Eggplant, Zucchini, and Onion Roast with Goat Cheese

Continuing with my roasting theme, we now take a detour to the Mediterranean with this robust vegetable blend. I added a touch of balsamic vinegar to give the recipe a tangy finish and then I balanced that with some fresh basil at the end. Cooking is just a chemistry class in which you're trying to balance the sugar and acidity, much like making the perfect wine.

Serves 6 to 8

3	baby eggplants, cubed	*2*
1	bulb fennel, cut into 1/4-in/5-mm wedges	*1*
2	medium zucchini, cubed	*2*
2	large onions, sliced	*2*
1	red pepper, cut into squares	*1*
5	cloves garlic, unpeeled	*5*
3 tbsp	olive oil	*45 mL*
1 tbsp	balsamic vinegar	*15 mL*
	Salt and freshly cracked black pepper, to taste	
	Several sprigs fresh thyme	
4 oz	firm goat cheese, crumbled	*114 g*
	Fresh basil (for garnish)	

Preheat oven to 190°C (375°F).

Combine all ingredients, except basil and cheese, in medium bowl and toss until well coated.

Transfer to large roasting or gratin pan so that vegetables are hardly overlapping. Roast for 20 minutes, stirring often, until vegetables are just tender. Sprinkle with goat cheese and continue to roast for 5 to 8 minutes, or until cheese is golden and soft.

Remove from oven and sprinkle with basil and more pepper.

PREP

- This recipe can be easily adjusted to smaller amounts; simply make sure you use a smaller roasting pan. The trick is to have enough space so the veggies don't overlap, but not too much so that they burn.

OPTIONS

- Also works very well as a summer salad served at room temperature.
- Toss any leftovers on prepared pasta for a quick sauce.

Colourful Stuffed Peppers

Serves 6

Although this recipe seems to have a million ingredients, it's still very simple and is a vegetarian's dream. You will get flavour, protein, and colour from this delicious blend. You can always trim it down to suit your needs, but this gives you an idea of how interesting vegetables actually can be.

PREP

- Because this is a vegetarian rice dish, the many ingredients and spices help to give it a very interesting flavour. When you put the peppers in the oven to roast, organize the remaining ingredients, get the rice going, and it will come together nicely.

- These will keep in the fridge for a couple of days and you can reheat them in the microwave. The rice will lose some texture, but the flavour will actually improve.

OPTIONS

- You can omit any of the nuts, seeds, or raisins in this recipe, but you will lose texture and protein.

- If you use only brown rice, try a medium-grain or long-grain brown rice, but adjust for the quantity of liquid and cooking time.

2	each red, yellow, and green peppers	2
1/4 cup	olive oil	50 mL
	Salt and pepper, to taste	
1	small onion, finely chopped	1
3	cloves garlic, chopped	3
1/2	each red pepper and yellow pepper, finely diced	1/2
	Zest of 1 lemon, grated	
1/2 tsp	ground coriander seed	2 mL
1/2 tsp	fennel seed, ground	2 mL
1/4 cup	almonds, chopped	50 mL
2 cups	vegetable stock	500 mL
Pinch	cayenne pepper	Pinch
3/4 cup	short-grain rice	175 mL
1/4 cup	red lentils	50 mL
1/4 cup	chopped fresh mint	50 mL
4	green onions, chopped	4
1/2 cup	green peas	125 mL
1/4 cup	each diced dried apricots and golden raisins	50 mL

Preheat oven to 180°C (350°F). Cut the tops off the peppers. Remove seeds and rinse. Place on baking sheet with 15 mL (1 tbsp) olive oil. Replace tops of peppers. Cover with foil and bake for 35 to 40 minutes, or until peppers are tender but not soft. Season with salt and pepper. Cool slightly.

Meanwhile, to prepare rice, sauté onion, garlic, and peppers on medium heat in remaining olive oil for about 5 minutes, or until onions are soft. Add lemon zest, coriander, fennel, and almonds. Sauté for 3 minutes.

Add stock and cayenne and stir again. Bring to a boil and add rice. Cover and reduce heat to low. Simmer for 10 to 15 minutes, or until rice just begins to soften but all water has not been absorbed. Remove from heat immediately.

Meanwhile, rinse lentils. Drain. Cook in boiling water in a small pot for 3 to 5 minutes, or until just tender. Drain and add to rice. Add mint, green onions, peas, apricots, and raisins and stir.

Fill the peppers and replace tops. Cover again tightly with foil and bake for 20 minutes, or until peppers are completely tender.

Sautéed Beet Greens

This is the ideal recipe to prepare when you buy beets and you don't know what to do with the greens. In Europe, the greens are never wasted. Their flavour resembles that of Swiss chard, and they are ultra-simple to prepare.

1 tsp	vegetable oil	5 mL
1	bunch beet greens, well washed and chopped, stems included	1
	Salt and freshly cracked black pepper, to taste	
1 tbsp	sesame seeds	15 mL
2 tbsp	plum vinegar	30 mL

In large skillet, heat oil on high. Add beet greens and toss quickly until just wilted, about 3 minutes or until stems begin to soften. Remove from heat and season. Add sesame seeds and plum vinegar.

Serves 4 to 6

PREP
- When selecting beets, look for greens with unblemished leaves that aren't wilted.

OPTIONS
- Use apple cider vinegar or rice wine vinegar if you can't find plum vinegar.
- Swiss chard can be substituted for the beet greens.

For the Birds

Best-Ever Roasted Chicken

Serves 4

PREP

- The simplest way to truss a bird is to cut a piece of twine about 45 cm (18 in) long. Lay the twine horizontally in front of you. Place bird on top of the twine with legs towards you and twine resting about 5 cm (2 in) from neck. Lift both sides of twine towards you, following the space between legs and breast. Wrap the twine around the bottoms of the legs, crossing them and tying the two pieces of twine together as tightly as possible. This helps keep the shape of the bird while roasting and ensures even cooking.

- When selecting a chicken do not use cheap, old birds for roasting purposes. They will never be tender unless you stew them for hours. I always suggest that people buy premium grain-fed chicken where possible. Let's face it: For the price of a couple of cappuccinos, you can have delicious chicken instead of a mass-produced one. The choice is yours.

A simple roasted chicken can be so incredible or it can be a dry, tasteless waste of time. This recipe will ensure your success from this day forward in roasting chicken. You need to start with a good-quality fresh chicken for this to work. The lemon and sage leaves placed between the skin and flesh add visual interest as well as incredible flavour. The wild mushroom sauce is optional, but you'll find it's so simple to make you may want to use it all the time.

1	roasting chicken (about 2-1/2 to 3 lb/1.14 to 1.4 kg)	*1*
1	lemon	*1*
	Several leaves fresh sage	
	Salt and freshly cracked black pepper, to taste	
1 tbsp	olive oil	*15 mL*

Sauce

2 tbsp	butter	*30 mL*
4	shallots, sliced	*4*
3	Portobello mushrooms, cut in large cubes	*3*
1	clove garlic, chopped	*1*
1/4 cup	port	*50 mL*
1/2 cup	chicken stock	*125 mL*
1/2 cup	dry red wine	*125 mL*
1/2 tsp	cornstarch	*2 mL*
1 tsp	cold water	*5 mL*

Preheat oven to 190°C (375°F).

Rub chicken with juice of 1/2 lemon and cut remaining lemon into slices. Stuff cavity of chicken with lemon slices and half the sage. Place fingers between skin and flesh on both neck and bottom sides of chicken. Gently slide fingers under, pulling the skin away from meat. Lay remainder of sage in a decorative pattern flat under skin. Season with salt and pepper and rub skin with olive oil. Truss chicken with butcher's twine and roast in medium roasting pan for 45 minutes to 1 hour, or until juice no longer runs pink and skin is crisp and browned.

Meanwhile, sauté shallots in butter on high heat in medium saucepan for 3 minutes, or until golden and soft. Reduce heat to medium high, add mushrooms, and sauté until brown, about 3 minutes. Add garlic and sauté for 1 minute. Add port and reduce for 1 minute. Add stock and red wine and bring to a boil. Reduce for 10 minutes, or until dark and reduced by half. Combine cornstarch and cold water and stir. Add to sauce and stir until thickened and boiling. Remove from heat and serve with chicken.

PREP

- Do not add liquid to your roasting pan, as this starts to steam the chicken. You want a dry roasting method.

OPTIONS

- If you're in a hurry, you can chop the sage and sprinkle it on top of the bird instead of laying it under the skin.
- Thyme, rosemary, or marjoram can be used instead of sage.

Grilled Chicken Breast
in Creamy Tarragon Wine Sauce

Serves 4

This is an unusual combination of a simple grilled chicken breast paired with a white wine cream sauce. The marriage of the grilled chicken and the sweet cream and white wine is fabulous and takes very little preparation. The sauce is a classical French reduction that intensifies flavour.

1 tsp	butter	*5 mL*
1	onion, chopped	*1*
1/2 cup	chicken stock	*125 mL*
1/2 cup	dry white wine	*125 mL*
1/2 cup	35% cream	*125 mL*
1 tbsp	fresh tarragon, chopped	*15 mL*
	Salt and freshly cracked black pepper, to taste	
4	boneless, skinless chicken breasts	*4*

PREP

• You never want to use a wine that you would not drink in a sauce. It doesn't have to be expensive wine, but it should be dry.

• Start grilling the chicken when you add the cream to the sauce and your timing will be perfect.

OPTION

• If you want a taste of this creamy sauce but you don't want the fat, try using a light (5%) cream. Mix it cold with 5 mL (1 tsp) of cornstarch and blend until smooth. Then add it to the sauce. If you don't use cornstarch, the sauce will split.

Heat butter in medium saucepan on high. Add onion and sauté for 3 minutes. Add stock and white wine. Reduce heat to minimum and simmer for 15 minutes, or until reduced by half. Add cream and tarragon and simmer uncovered until slightly thickened, about 10 minutes. Season with salt and pepper.

Meanwhile, grill chicken breasts on a hot grill that has been oiled and well brushed. Season with salt and pepper and grill for 6 minutes on each side, or until juices run clear and meat is no longer pink. Pour sauce over chicken and serve with your favourite vegetables.

Chicken and Black Bean Quesadilla

These tortillas are a fun, different way to use chicken. They're also a good way to sneak some healthy beans in for the kids. Serve with some veggies and a simple salad. These are also perfect as appetizers if you use smaller tortillas.

Serves 4

4	chicken breasts, boneless, skinless	4
	Salt and pepper, to taste	
1	small chipotle chile, soaked in hot water, then finely chopped	1
1/2 tsp	cumin seed, cracked	2 mL
2 tsp	vegetable oil	10 mL
2/3 cup	cooked black beans (or 1 small can, drained)	150 mL
1	red pepper, diced	1
1/4 cup	chopped fresh parsley	50 mL
	Fresh coriander (optional)	
3	green onions, chopped	3
4	8-in/20-cm flour or corn tortillas	4
1/4 cup	grated Monterey Jack cheese	50 mL
	Fresh tomatoes, diced	

Preheat oven to 190°C (375°F).

Rub chicken with salt, pepper, 1/2 of chipotle, and cumin seed. In medium saucepan, heat vegetable oil over high heat and sear chicken 3 minutes on each side, until golden. Remove pan from heat and transfer chicken to a roasting pan or skillet with heat-proof handle. Finish cooking chicken in oven for 8 to 10 minutes, or until juices run clear.

Meanwhile, return pan to heat. Over medium heat, toss remaining chipotle with beans and red pepper and stir with wooden spoon for 2 minutes. Add chopped parsley, coriander, and green onions. Remove from heat. Season to taste.

To assemble, slice chicken into thirds on the bias. Lay tortilla on board. Sprinkle with 1/4 of cheese. Arrange chicken on top in a single layer (using 2 chicken breasts per tortilla). Sprinkle with bean mixture and cover with 1/4 of the cheese and some tomatoes. Top with another tortilla. Repeat with other tortillas, creating 2 sandwiches.

Bake for 8 to 10 minutes, until golden, turning once. Cut into wedges.

PREP

- The filling for these tortillas can be made in advance and then assembled just before serving.

- If you use corn tortillas instead of flour, the texture will be a little tougher and chewy.

OPTIONS

- You can change the filling to just about anything. Just be sure to keep the cheese, because that holds it all together.

- Use cheddar, Gouda, or fontina instead of Monterey Jack.

- For an appetizer, use 15-cm (6-in) tortillas. You will probably get 4 sandwiches out of the filling.

Grilled Chicken Wrapped in Tortilla with Chipotle Sour Cream

Serves 4

Ever since I made this recipe on the show I have had numerous requests for more information on chipotles. They are simply smoked and dried jalapeño chiles, and they have been used in Mexico for many years. They generally add a spicy yet smoky edge to a dish, in this case to the sour cream. These wraps are packed with flavour and can be made with a variety of tortillas to add variety in colour, taste, and textures.

2	medium chicken breasts, skinless, boneless	2
2 tsp	vegetable oil	10 mL
	Zest of 1 lime, grated	
	Juice of 1 lime	
1 tsp	Dijon mustard	5 mL
1 tsp	chopped fresh coriander	5 mL
	Salt and freshly cracked black pepper, to taste	
1/4 cup	sour cream	50 mL
1	small chipotle chile, soaked and minced	1
4	6-in/15-cm soft flour tortillas	4
	Red Oak leaf lettuce (for garnish)	
	Red onion, finely sliced (for garnish)	

Heat barbecue on high. Brush grill well to prevent sticking.

Meanwhile combine oil, lime zest and juice, mustard, and coriander and brush over chicken. Season with salt and pepper.

Grill on medium-high heat for 6 minutes per side, or until juices run clear. Cool slightly. Combine sour cream and chipotle until blended.

To assemble, slice chicken. Roll tortillas into a cone and pinch bottom end. Fill with lettuce, chicken, and onion, drizzle with sour cream, and place on plate seam side down to prevent opening.

PREP

- Ideally, wraps should be assembled while chicken is still warm, although they could be assembled with cold chicken. You will lose a little juice and flavour, though.
- Any leftover chipotle sour cream can be kept covered in the fridge and used on baked potatoes or sandwiches.

OPTIONS

- Chicken can be cooked in the oven if a barbecue is not available.
- Fresh Atlantic salmon is also delicious in this recipe instead of chicken.

Stir-Fried Chicken with Pineapple and Red Pepper

This is a great everyday stir-fry that you can make with your eyes closed. Well, maybe you'd better try it once with them open, then slowly close them. This recipe has all the popular features of sweet and sour Chinese take-out without all of the artificial colour and additives. And the added bonus is that you can use all the vegetables you want.

Serves 4

2	chicken breasts, skinless, boneless	2
3 tbsp	vegetable oil	45 mL
1	medium onion, chopped	1
1	clove garlic, chopped	1
1 tsp	fresh ginger, chopped	5 mL
1/2 tsp	fresh jalapeño chile, chopped	2 mL
1	red pepper, chopped	1
1/2	fresh pineapple, cubed	1/2
1/4 cup	teriyaki sauce	50 mL
1 tbsp	honey	15 mL
	Juice of 1 lime	
	Juice of 1/2 lemon	
	Salt, to taste	

Slice chicken into thin strips.

Heat 1/2 the oil in wok over high heat. Place chicken in hot wok and toss until cooked through (about 4 minutes). Remove and set aside.

Pour remaining oil into wok and place over high heat until very hot. Add onion, garlic, ginger, and jalapeño and toss for 3 minutes. Add remaining ingredients and cook for 3 minutes. Add chicken, just to heat through. Serve over Thai jasmine or basmati rice.

PREP

- As always when stir-frying, chop all vegetables and chicken before heating the wok.
- Make sure you cook the chicken all the way through before removing it from the wok initially. When you add it back, you just want to heat it through. This prevents the chicken from drying out by being in the pan too long.

OPTIONS

- You can use canned, no-sugar-added pineapple, although fresh will provide the best results.
- You can replace the jalapeño with dried chiles. Start with 1 mL (1/4 tsp) of dried chile. Then, if you want more spice, add away. You can always add, but you can never get rid of too much spice.

Chicken Breast Scallopini with Chorizo Tomato Sauce

Serves 4 to 6

This recipe gets top marks for colour, texture, flavour, and simplicity. At first I was just looking for an alternative to veal scallopini, but when I added pecorino cheese to the breading and chorizo sausage to the sauce this dish came to life.

1 cup	breadcrumbs	*250 mL*
1/2 cup	grated pecorino cheese	*125 mL*
2	sprigs fresh thyme, leaves only, chopped	*2*
	Salt and freshly cracked black pepper, to taste	
8	pieces of chicken breast scallopini, thinly sliced (3 oz/85 g each)	*8*
2	eggs, whisked with fork	*2*
2 tbsp	olive oil	*30 mL*

Sauce

1 tbsp	olive oil	*15 mL*
1	large onion, chopped	*1*
3	cloves garlic, finely chopped	*3*
1	chorizo sausage, casing removed and crumbled	*1*
1	large can (28 oz/795 g) plum tomatoes	*1*
2	large sprigs fresh thyme	*2*
1 tsp	dried oregano	*5 mL*

To prepare the sauce, heat olive oil in medium saucepan and sauté onion on high heat for 3 minutes. Add garlic and toss for 2 minutes until both are soft. Add sausage and brown for 1 minute. Add tomatoes and herbs and bring to a boil. Reduce to low heat and simmer uncovered for 20 to 30 minutes, or until sauce is thick.

Meanwhile, combine breadcrumbs, cheese, and thyme in shallow baking pan or aluminum tin and season. Dip chicken in egg and then in breadcrumb mixture, coating well. Lay on baking sheet. Separate layers of chicken with waxed paper or parchment paper. Cover with plastic wrap and refrigerate until ready to cook.

Fry chicken in olive oil in large skillet on medium-high heat. Cook 2 to 3 pieces at a time, depending on size of pan. Fry for 3 to 4 minutes per side, until browned on both sides and no longer pink. Cut a little piece off to ensure it's cooked.

PREP

- Adding cheese to the breading will make the scallopini brown a little more quickly. Make sure you cook the chicken all the way through.

- Scallopini are also called cutlets. If your butcher does not sell chicken that way, you can ask him or her to slice some chicken breast thinly for you. To flatten cutlets, cover with plastic wrap and use a mallet or rolling pin to ensure even thickness.

OPTIONS

- Chorizo is a spicy Latin sausage that is available at most Spanish or Latin grocery stores. If you can't find it, substitute a spicy Italian sausage.

- Pecorino (Italian sheep's milk cheese) is available at any specialty cheese shop. You can use Parmesan cheese instead of pecorino.

Chicken Chasseur

This is my variation on an ancient French recipe known as "hunter's style." Don't fear: The most you have to do is brave the traffic and maybe a check-out line to purchase the chicken. This stew has an aromatic woody sauce with wild mushrooms, brandy, tomatoes, and tarragon. The use of boneless chicken legs makes for a simple stew with great flavour that cooks fairly quickly.

1-1/2 tbsp	olive oil	*22 mL*
6	chicken legs, skinless, boneless	*6*
1	medium onion, chopped	*1*
1	large clove garlic, chopped	*1*
1/2	red pepper, chopped	*1/2*
3	shiitake mushrooms, sliced	*3*
2	Portobello mushrooms, sliced	*2*
1/4 cup	dry white wine	*50 mL*
1/4 cup	brandy	*50 mL*
1	small can (14 oz/398 g) plum tomatoes with juice	*1*
2	sprigs thyme	*2*
1	bay leaf	*1*
	Salt and pepper, to taste	
1 tbsp	fresh tarragon	*15 mL*

In medium saucepan, heat oil over high heat, add chicken, and brown evenly, about 5 minutes. Remove and set aside.

If there is no oil left in the pan, add 5 mL (1 tsp) or so. Reduce heat to medium and add onion, garlic, and red pepper. Cook, stirring frequently, until mixture softens, about 4 minutes. Add mushrooms and sauté for 3 minutes over medium heat, or until golden. Add back chicken and white wine, brandy, tomatoes, thyme, and bay leaf. Reduce heat to low and simmer, uncovered, for 30 minutes, or until chicken is tender. Season with salt and pepper.

Add tarragon and simmer for 5 minutes.

Serves 4 to 6

PREP

- If you can't find boneless chicken legs, use thighs or drumsticks and thighs with the bone in. Actually, you get much better flavour with the bone in, but it takes a little longer to cook and is messy to eat.

- This dish can be frozen or kept covered in the fridge for a couple of days.

- The tarragon is added at the very end or it will lose its flavour.

OPTIONS

- The fresh mushrooms can be replaced with dried chanterelles, porcini, or other intense mushrooms. Wash them and soak in hot water for about 20 minutes to plump them up. A little goes a long way, so one small package will suffice. I would still use some fresh mushrooms to complement the dried ones.

- When you have more time on a weekend, try this stew with lamb shoulder.

Chicken Pot au Feu

Serves 4 to 6

I call this my one-pot wonder because all ingredients are simply added in sequence to the same pot. In the past, a traditional *pot au feu* (pot on fire) was cooked on an open fire and usually used a tough cut of beef that was cooked all day long. If we could only have that much time to make dinner. With this recipe you get the essence of a *pot au feu* with plenty of time to spare.

1 tbsp	olive oil	*15 mL*
4	chicken legs, cut in half	*4*
2	medium onions, chopped	*2*
2	large cloves garlic, chopped	*2*
1/4 cup	flour	*50 mL*
3	large carrots, cubed	*3*
3	medium new potatoes, quartered	*3*
2	stalks celery, diced	*2*
4	plum tomatoes, diced (fresh or canned)	*4*
3 cups	chicken stock	*750 mL*
1/2 cup	dry white wine	*125 mL*
	Zest of 1 lemon, grated	
1	bulb fennel, diced	*1*
2	large sprigs fresh thyme	*2*
1	sprig fresh rosemary, chopped	*1*
1 tsp	dried oregano	*5 mL*
2	large bay leaves	*2*
	Salt and freshly cracked black pepper, to taste	
	Fresh parsley, chopped, to taste	

PREP

- The parsley should be added just before serving or it will lose its flavour and turn brown.
- This is another great dish that can be covered and refrigerated for a couple of days.

OPTION

- To reduce the fat, remove the skin from the chicken before browning.

In large casserole, heat half the oil on high. Dredge chicken pieces in flour. Brown on high heat evenly on both sides, turning once. Remove pan from heat and remove chicken pieces. Add remaining olive oil, onions, and garlic and sauté for 5 minutes, until soft. Add remaining ingredients and browned chicken pieces and bring to a boil. Cover and simmer on low heat for 25 to 30 minutes, or until chicken is tender. Season with salt and pepper and sprinkle with parsley just before serving.

Chicken with Celery and Leeks in Egg Lemon Sauce

This recipe uses a preparation called "avgolemono" that is one of the most popular in Greece. Most often it is part of a tangy chicken and rice soup that I was raised on. Here it adds that lemony zip to a simple stew. If you were to use lamb instead of chicken, the flavour would be more pronounced but you would need more time for slow simmering. See the Prep section for tips on mastering the egg lemon sauce.

Serves 4 to 6

3 tbsp	olive oil	*45 mL*
1	large onion, chopped	*1*
2	leeks, white part only, washed and sliced	*2*
6	chicken thighs, skinless, boneless	*6*
4	stalks celery, sliced	*4*
3 cups	chicken stock	*750 mL*
	Salt and pepper, to taste	
2	eggs, separated	*2*
	Juice of 1 lemon	
1 tbsp	chopped fresh dill (for garnish)	*15 mL*
2	green onions, chopped	*2*

In large skillet, heat olive oil on high heat and sauté onions and leeks until soft, about 5 to 6 minutes. Add chicken pieces and turn often until evenly browned. Add celery and 500 mL (2 cups) of stock. Bring to a boil. Reduce to simmer and cover for 20 to 25 minutes, or until chicken is tender. Adjust seasoning. Keep on a low simmer.

Bring remaining stock to a gentle simmer in small pot.

Meanwhile, in medium bowl, whisk together egg yolks and lemon juice until smooth. When pot of broth is simmering, pour it slowly into egg mixture in a steady stream, while whisking vigorously.

In a separate medium bowl, whisk egg whites until light and frothy, about 1 minute. Fold into hot egg mixture.

Pour tempered egg mixture over chicken while stirring, then remove from heat immediately. Sprinkle with dill and green onions. Serve with pita or crusty bread.

PREP

• The tricky part of this recipe is the egg lemon sauce. You want to heat the egg mixture enough to cook it, but you don't want it to scramble. The small pot of stock simmering is a good trick. Once you've tempered the egg yolks (by adding the hot stock gradually) and folded in the egg whites, you want the chicken to be on a low simmer. Pour the egg mixture over the chicken all at once while stirring and remove it immediately from heat. The eggs will cook from the residual heat.

• When reheating in the microwave, the eggs will cook, but this won't alter the taste.

OPTION

• The chicken can be replaced by lamb shoulder, but this requires a longer cooking time.

Lemongrass Ginger Seared Chicken Breast

Serves 4

Flavour, flavour, flavour comes to mind when I think of this recipe. It's a simple combination of lemongrass and coconut milk, with a few other goodies thrown in for fun. The black sesame seed crust provides flavour and great texture. If you refer to the Mise en Place chapter, you'll notice that many of these ingredients are listed as good additions to your pantry. After trying this recipe, you'll know why.

2	cloves garlic, minced	*2*
1 tsp	black sesame seeds	*5 mL*
1	small Thai chile, finely chopped	*1*
1 tbsp	chopped fresh ginger	*15 mL*
4	boneless, skinless chicken breasts (about 5 oz/142 g each)	*4*
	Salt, to taste	
1 tbsp	vegetable oil	*15 mL*
2	stalks lemongrass, white part only, chopped	*2*
1/2 cup	white wine	*125 mL*
3/4 cup	coconut milk	*175 mL*

Combine garlic, sesame seeds, chile, and 1/2 the ginger and stir until blended.

Rub over chicken. Season with salt. In large skillet, heat oil on high. Sear chicken 3 minutes per side, or until golden. Remove from skillet and transfer to baking pan.

Preheat oven to 180°C (350°F).

Return skillet to heat and add remaining ginger and lemongrass. Sauté for 2 minutes, or until ginger is golden. Add white wine and coconut milk and reduce heat to low. Simmer for 8 to 10 minutes, or until sauce is slightly thickened.

Meanwhile, bake chicken in oven for 10 minutes, or until juices run clear. Immediately lay in pan with coconut sauce.

Serve over cooked jasmine rice.

PREP

- Once the chicken is fully cooked in the oven, you only want to lay it in the sauce to absorb some flavour, not to boil it to death. Chicken breast should be tender and moist.

OPTIONS

- If you want to decrease the fat by about 60 percent, substitute 125 mL (1/2 cup) chicken stock for the coconut milk. Then, just before serving, blend 30 mL (2 tbsp) cold light coconut milk with 5 mL (1 tsp) cornstarch. Whisk the mixture into boiling sauce and bring to a boil. Sauce will have a slightly thick consistency.

- You can use dried lemongrass or grated lemon zest if fresh lemongrass is not available. Check availability at Thai specialty stores.

Chicken with Brie, Apples, and Sage

A great way to add sophistication to chicken breast is to stuff it. This dish is a beautiful combination of creamy Brie, tart apples, shallots and garlic. The pancetta (Italian bacon) secures the filling and gives the chicken a crisp, smoky crust. It's a little tricky to stuff, but if you follow my guidelines you should have no problems.

Serves 4

1 tsp	butter *5 mL*	
1	each large shallot and clove garlic, finely chopped *1*	
1	small apple (preferably Matsu or Granny Smith), peeled and chopped *1*	
1 tsp	chopped fresh sage *5 mL*	
2 oz	Brie cheese, crumbled *57 g*	
	Salt and pepper, to taste	
4	chicken breasts, boneless, skinless *4*	
1	egg white *1*	
8	slices pancetta *8*	
1 tbsp	vegetable oil *15 mL*	

Preheat oven to 190°C (375°F).

In medium saucepan, heat butter over high heat. Add shallot and garlic and stir with wooden spoon for 2 minutes, or until translucent. Add apple and continue to cook until slightly soft. Add sage and remove from heat. Cool. Combine apple mixture with cheese and season with salt and pepper. Stir well with wooden spoon until combined.

Make a vertical slit in the bottom of each chicken breast, running the length of the breast but not through it. Imagine a three-dimensional "T" shape that creates a pocket but does not come through the other side of the breast.

Fill each breast with 30-45 mL (2-3 tbsp) of stuffing. Brush chicken with egg white where slit has been made. Sprinkle with salt and pepper and some more sage, if desired, then wrap each breast with 2 slices of pancetta. Toothpicks can be used to fasten pancetta.

In medium skillet, heat vegetable oil on high heat and add chicken breasts, slit facing down. Brown for 2 minutes, turn over, and repeat on other side. Remove skillet from heat. Transfer breasts to roasting pan and finish cooking in oven for 15 minutes, or until firm when pressed down. You may need to cut the edge of a piece of chicken to ensure that the meat is cooked.

PREP

- When slitting the chicken breasts, avoid cutting them in half, because the filling will run out during baking. If you use a small paring knife or a sharp boning knife, you can create a pocket for the filling as described in the recipe.

- The egg white helps to seal the slit when baked.

- The cheese and apple in the filling give you a little more moisture, so it's difficult to overcook the chicken. However, don't cook it for more than 20 minutes.

OPTIONS

- For a low-fat version of this recipe, eliminate the cheese.

- To fasten the pancetta, you also can wrap with pieces of butcher's twine before searing.

Jerked Chicken Skewers with Fruit Sauce

Serves 4

This is a variation on my other jerk recipe (see Jerked Swordfish Skewers with Red Lentils on page 122). The fruit sauce is a good way to cool the palette after the blistering attack of spice from the rub. If you want to try the jerk rub but don't want all that heat, simply reduce the chile to 1/4 of a whole scotch bonnet.

Spice rub

1	bunch fresh thyme, leaves only, chopped	*1*
1/2	bunch green onions, finely chopped	*1/2*
2 tbsp	chopped fresh ginger	*30 mL*
2	cloves garlic, minced	*2*
	Juice of 1/2 lime	
1-2	large scotch bonnet chiles, stemmed and finely chopped	*1-2*
1 tsp	ground allspice	*5 mL*
1/2 tsp	ground cinnamon	*2 mL*
1-1/2 tsp	ground coriander seed	*7 mL*
1 tsp	freshly cracked pepper	*5 mL*
1/4 cup	vegetable oil	*50 mL*
3 tbsp	orange juice	*45 mL*

Combine all ingredients and stir well. Store in sealed container in fridge until ready to use.

Chicken

4	medium chicken breasts, boneless, skinless, sliced into thin strips	*4*
	Salt, to taste	

Using about 125 mL (1/2 cup) of spice mixture, marinate chicken slices in shallow container, covering well with rub for as long as 6 hours. Remove from marinade and thread onto wooden skewers that have been soaked in water for 30 minutes. Season with salt and grill for 3 to 4 minutes per side.

PREP

- See recipe notes on Jerked Swordfish Skewers with Red Lentils (page 122).
- You can prepare the rub, use what you can, and then freeze the remainder, since it is difficult to make very small quantities. It will also keep in the fridge for several days.

Fruit Sauce

1	small mango, finely diced	*1*
1	small papaya, finely diced	*1*
1	kiwi, finely diced	*1*
	Juice of 1 lime	
1	small red onion, finely diced	*1*
1/4 cup	fresh orange juice	*50 mL*

Combine all ingredients until blended. Remove half and purée in food processor. Return to mixture and stir to combine. Store in fridge until ready to use.

OPTION

• If you omit the onion, the fruit sauce can be tossed in a blender with some ice for a great tropical drink. Add a paper umbrella and you've got a little escape.

Ultimate Club Sandwich

Makes 2 sandwiches

The original recipe is a retro favourite, but I'm giving it a 1990s facelift. It made the "Dish It Out" crew's top 10 recipe list. I'm using pancetta instead of regular bacon, saffron aïoli for mayonnaise, and arugula instead of lettuce. To make it even more cosmopolitan, I'm adding tomato and eggplant relish. This is a great recipe to feature at a retro party or lunch, because people would never imagine that a sandwich could make such a splash. But remember: I'm giving you all the bells and whistles. Don't feel that you have to make the sandwich exactly as I describe.

6	thick slices good-quality, whole-grain bread, toasted 6
	Saffron aïoli (recipe follows)
2	roasted chicken breasts (preferably leftover) 2
4	thin slices pancetta (or bacon) 4
	Tomato and eggplant relish (recipe follows)
2	slices of tomato 2
	Several leaves arugula (or spinach), washed and dried

Assemble each sandwich by spreading some aïoli on a slice of bread, then stacking on top some chicken, 2 slices of pancetta, a second slice of bread, some relish, more chicken, 1 slice of tomato, some arugula, and a final slice of bread.

Saffron Aïoli

1-2	cloves garlic	1-2
Pinch	salt	Pinch
1	egg yolk	1
	Juice of 1/2 lemon	
Pinch	saffron	Pinch
Pinch	cayenne	Pinch
1/2 cup	olive oil	125 mL

Crush garlic and place in food processor. Add salt, egg yolk, lemon juice, saffron, and cayenne. Pulse to combine ingredients.

In a steady stream, add olive oil slowly through spout with machine on until mixture is smooth. Store covered in fridge until ready to use.

OPTIONS

• Regular bacon can be used in place of pancetta, or can be omitted altogether.

• For a lighter sandwich, eliminate the aïoli and pancetta.

PREP

• Everyone wants the official scoop on eating raw eggs. Here are my suggestions: There is never a 100-percent guarantee, but buy fresh eggs (check the dates). Don't store eggs in the fridge door (not cold enough). Always store mayonnaise in fridge before and after using. Never use broken or cracked eggs when making mayonnaise.

• If you feel safer using store-bought mayonnaise, simply add garlic and saffron to simulate the flavour of the aïoli.

Tomato and Eggplant Relish

1 tbsp	olive oil *15 mL*
1	large sweet onion (Vidalia or Spanish), finely diced *1*
1	small eggplant, finely diced *1*
1	yellow pepper, finely diced *1*
	Salt and freshly cracked black pepper, to taste
2	sprigs fresh thyme, chopped (or 1/2 tsp/2 mL dried) *2*
1/2 tsp	dried oregano *2 mL*
2	large roma tomatoes, diced *2*
1 tbsp	red wine vinegar *15 mL*
	Several leaves fresh basil, chopped

In large skillet, heat half the olive oil and sauté onion on medium-high heat. Continue to cook for 8 to 10 minutes until onion is soft and golden. Remove onion and reserve. In same skillet, heat remaining olive oil and sauté eggplant until golden and soft, about 3 to 4 minutes, tossing often to prevent burning. Add yellow pepper, cooked onions, spices (except basil), and tomatoes. Cook for 5 minutes, or until mixture is thick and juice has evaporated. Add vinegar and remove from heat. Stir in basil.

Vietnamese Chicken Curry

Serves 4

Vietnamese curries differ from most other Indian or Thai curries in that they are flavourful but not hot and spicy. Once you get the hang of making curries, you'll find that you improvise with all kinds of ingredients. Any curry dish simply needs steamed rice on the side.

1 tbsp	vegetable oil	*15 mL*
4	chicken thighs, boneless, skinless	*4*
2	large onions, chopped	*2*
5	shallots, chopped	*5*
3	cloves garlic, chopped	*3*
1 tbsp	chopped fresh ginger	*30 mL*
4	stalks lemongrass, minced	*4*
2	small Thai chiles, finely chopped	*2*
1 tbsp	mild, good-quality Indian curry powder	*15 mL*
1-1/2 tsp	coriander seeds, crushed	*7 mL*
3/4 cup	coconut milk	*175 mL*
2-3/4 cups	chicken stock	*675 mL*

Heat oil on high in medium saucepan. Add chicken and brown until golden, 3 to 5 minutes. Add onion, shallots, garlic, ginger, lemongrass, and chiles and sauté for several minutes, until soft. Add curry powder and coriander and toss until combined. Add coconut milk and stock. Bring to a boil. Stir and reduce heat to low.

Cover and simmer for 35 to 45 minutes, stirring occasionally, until chicken is tender.

Serve over steamed rice.

PREP

- You'll find it easier to eat any stewed dish when you use boneless chicken. To get more flavour, you can use dark meat with the bone in.

OPTIONS

- Coconut milk is the fat culprit in this recipe, so you can get rid of it if you want. However, the complexity of flavours will not be the same if you do.
- This same sauce can be used with shrimp, but don't cook the shrimp for more than a few minutes.

Turkey and Mushroom Burgers

Just when you thought turkey was only for Thanksgiving, you can make these burgers any time of year with ease. The mushroom, herb, and onion mixture that is ground right into the meat adds moisture and a very earthy component to the predictable flavour of turkey. As a more casual Thanksgiving option, these burgers are perfect because I have garnished them with maple-grilled squash and cranberry sauce. They're so good they even taste great at room temperature.

3 tbsp	butter	*45 mL*
1	small onion, coarsely chopped	*1*
2	Portobello mushrooms, diced	*2*
2	cloves garlic, chopped	*2*
1	egg	*1*
1 lb	ground turkey	*454 g*
	Salt and pepper, to taste	
2 tbsp	chopped fresh rosemary	*30 mL*
1/2 tsp	chopped fresh sage	*2 mL*
6	slices pepper squash, peeled, sliced, and blanched	*6*
2 tbsp	maple syrup	*30 mL*
6	whole-grain buns or large rolls	*6*
	Cranberry sauce (for garnish)	

In a skillet, melt 15 mL (1 tbsp) of butter and sauté onion, mushrooms, and garlic until soft and golden, about 5 minutes. Remove from heat and cool slightly.

In a food processor, pulse mushroom mixture with egg and remaining butter (softened), until finely chopped. Combine mushroom mixture and turkey in medium bowl and stir well. Season with salt and pepper and add rosemary and sage. Form gently into 4 to 6 patties.

Grill burgers on high for 5 to 6 minutes per side, or until juices no longer run pink. Be sure to cook through. Brush squash with maple syrup and grill alongside burgers, if desired.

Serve in toasted buns garnished with grilled slices of squash and cranberry sauce, if desired.

Serves 4 to 6

PREP

- The potential problem with turkey burgers is that they can be dry and lack taste. I've added butter right into the meat along with the mushrooms and herbs. If you're watching your fat intake, you can eliminate this.

- Always use ground meat within one day of buying it. Once ground, meat deteriorates much more quickly.

OPTIONS

- The grilled squash and cranberry sauce are just options, but they do make these burgers irresistible.

- You can also serve these burgers with the tomato and eggplant relish from the Ultimate Club Sandwich recipe (see page 88).

Maple Soy Roasted Quail

Serves 4

I'm always striving to introduce you to interesting yet simple dishes. Quail definitely falls into that category. Most people either save it for a festive occasion or only order it at a restaurant. In fact, quail is quite easy to cook if you don't try to remove all the bones like most restaurant chefs do. They do that so you don't have to pick up the quail with your hands and fight with the bones. At home, I happen to like the adventure of eating quail with the bones in. I simply cut the bird in half and remove the backbone. I also consider this recipe to be a good example of Canadian cuisine, as the maple syrup and quail are indigenous to Quebec and Ontario. The cherry and Pinot Noir sauce will blow you away.

4	whole quails	*4*
2 tbsp	soy sauce	*30 mL*
1 tbsp	grated fresh ginger	*15 mL*
2	cloves garlic, finely minced	*2*
1/4 cup	maple syrup	*50 mL*
1 tsp	Dijon mustard	*5 mL*
2	sprigs fresh thyme, chopped	*2*
2	scallions, finely minced	*2*
1 tbsp	vegetable oil	*15 mL*
	Salt and freshly cracked pepper, to taste	

PREP

- Many ethnic or upscale grocers sell quail fresh or frozen, or check with your local butcher.
- Prepare and marinate the quail and then start the sauce. Once the sauce is ready you can cook the quail any time. I always add the pan drippings from the roasted quail to the sauce for a good flavour boost.

Slice quails in half, lengthwise, removing the backbone with cleaver or heavy shears. In medium bowl, combine remaining ingredients, except salt and pepper, and stir well. Add quail to bowl and toss well. Cover and chill for 30 minutes or as long as 2 hours.

Remove from fridge and season with salt and pepper. Cook quail on the grill on medium-high heat until crisp and evenly browned on all sides (about 3 to 4 minutes per side). Or, sear quail in hot skillet with 15 mL (1 tbsp) vegetable oil for 1 to 2 minutes per side, then transfer to oven and bake at 190°C (375°F) for 8 to 10 minutes, or until just pink in middle. Quail should not be served well done or it will dry out!

A simple yet elegant cherry sauce recipe follows, if you're in the mood.

Serve with couscous, potatoes, or rice and vegetables.

Cherry and Pinot Noir Sauce

1 tbsp	butter	*15 mL*
3	shallots, finely sliced	*3*
1/2 cup	Pinot Noir (or other fruity, rich red wine)	*125 mL*
1 cup	chicken stock	*250 mL*
2	sprigs fresh thyme	*2*
1	bay leaf	*1*
3/4 cup	bing cherries, pitted and cut in half	*175 mL*

In medium saucepan or skillet, sauté shallots in butter over medium heat for 3 to 4 minutes, or until soft. Add red wine, chicken stock, any pan drippings from the roasted quail, thyme, and bay leaf. Simmer uncovered until reduced by a third, about 8 to 10 minutes. Add cherries and simmer for 2 minutes, until just soft. Remove bay leaf and adjust seasoning. Serve over quail.

OPTION

- This recipe works in winter by substituting dried cherries for the fresh ones. Use only 125 mL (1/2 cup) dried cherries.

Wildflower Honey-Glazed Muscovy Duck Breast

Serves 4 to 6

PREP

- The Muscovy breed of duck, also called Barbary, has a leaner, larger breast that is quite tender and has great flavour. It is my favourite duck to cook. If you can't find it, ask your butcher for a local substitute. You need to adjust the cooking time since the breast can range in size from 227 to 454 g (1/2 to 1 lb).

- The breast meat is very lean if you remove the thick layer of fat. I would recommend cooking it as per recipe, then removing the fat layer, or the meat will be too dry.

- If duck breast is cooked well done, it is dry and tough. I prefer medium to medium rare.

- If you're making this dish for a party, you can rub the duck the day before and keep it covered in the fridge for up to 24 hours. Don't feel that you need to marinate the duck, but it can help the flavour. Some breeds are very gamy and soaking them in wine helps to round out that taste.

Duck is usually a festive bird, but when cooked whole it is quite wasteful, since you need two ducks to feed four people. Using just the breast is expensive, but your cooking time is quartered and you will have no waste. The rub of wildflower honey and Provencal herbs is delicious any time of year, but for the holidays try the tart, fruity cranberry pear sauce. Not only is this duck elegant but it looks incredible on the plate and you don't need a cooking school diploma to make it.

2	Muscovy duck breasts (about 1 lb/454 g each)	2
	Salt, to taste	
	Vegetable oil or clarified butter (for searing)	

Rub

	Zest of 1 lemon, grated	
	Juice of 1/2 lemon	
1 tbsp	wildflower or lavender honey	15 mL
2	cloves garlic, finely chopped	2
2 tbsp	herbes de Provence	30 mL
1/2 tsp	freshly cracked black pepper	2 mL
1 tsp	grated fresh ginger	5 mL

Combine all ingredients for rub in a small bowl. Rub thoroughly on both sides of duck breasts. Cover and refrigerate up to 24 hours.

Preheat oven to 180°C (350°F).

Score skin side of breasts with sharp knife. Season breast with salt. Meanwhile, heat a large ovenproof skillet or grill pan and add butter or oil. Sear breasts, skin side down, over moderate heat for about 5 minutes, or until well browned. Turn over and sear flesh side for 1 minute. Drain fat and discard.

Transfer duck to small roasting pan, skin side down, and continue cooking in oven for 10 to 14 minutes. Turn breasts over and cook other side for about 5 minutes. Flesh should start to feel a little firm when pressed down with spatula. Drain off some of the fat, if necessary. Remove from oven and let rest for at least 5 minutes, covered with foil. Slice very thinly.

Serve with pear and cranberry sauce, if desired (recipe follows).

Pear and Cranberry Sauce

1 tbsp	butter or vegetable oil	*15 mL*
4	shallots, finely sliced	*4*
1	large bosc or other firm ripe pear, peeled and diced	*1*
1/2 cup	chicken stock	*125 mL*
1/4 cup	cassis (black currant liqueur)	*50 mL*
1/2 cup	fresh or frozen cranberries	*125 mL*

In a medium saucepan, sauté shallots in butter for 3 to 5 minutes over high heat until soft and golden. Add pear and sauté for 1 minute, until just golden. Add remaining ingredients and bring to a boil. Reduce heat to medium and simmer uncovered until reduced by about one-third, about 10 minutes.

Serve with duck.

OPTIONS

- You can easily make this dish in the summer. Grill the duck on the barbecue and then finish it further from the heat on a higher rack to cook the middle without burning the skin. Serve it with a fresh berry sauce, such as blackberry and peach or blueberry. The duck simply needs a sweet, fruity accompaniment.

- Serve the pear and cranberry sauce with turkey or Cornish hen.

- Herbes de Provence is a blend of dried herbs. If you can't find it, use a blend of rosemary, thyme, lavender, and marjoram.

Sage and Garlic Roasted Cornish Hens with Cranberry Apricot Sauce

Serves 4

You will be truly amazed at how easy it is to make Cornish hens throughout the week. They have a more interesting gamy flavour than chickens do and, when cut in half, can be roasted in about 25 minutes. The other really cool thing about this recipe is the sauce. In summer I use fresh apricots and dried cranberries and in winter I use dried apricots and fresh cranberries. Isn't that a great twist? You don't need to announce to the kids that they aren't chickens either.

2	medium Cornish hens	2
	Salt and pepper, to taste	
	Juice of 1 lemon	
2	cloves garlic, minced	2
2 tbsp	chopped fresh sage	30 mL
1 tbsp	olive oil	15 mL

Sauce

1 cup	fresh or frozen cranberries	250 mL
1/4 cup	dried apricots, chopped	50 mL
1/4 cup	orange juice	50 mL
3 tbsp	brown sugar	45 mL

PREP
- Most good grocers or butchers have fresh Cornish hens around Christmas. During the rest of the year, you can buy them frozen.

OPTION
- If you don't mind a little more tang in your sauce, eliminate the brown sugar from the sauce or reduce it. We probably eat too much sugar anyway.

Preheat oven to 190°C (375°F). Heat empty large roasting pan in oven until hot.

Meanwhile, cut hens in half, lengthwise, with cleaver or kitchen shears. Season with salt and pepper and rub with lemon juice, garlic, sage, and half the olive oil.

Add remaining olive oil to hot pan and lay hens in, skin side down. Roast for 15 minutes and turn over. Roast 10 to 15 minutes, until golden and juices run clear.

Meanwhile, combine ingredients for sauce in small saucepan and bring to a boil. Reduce heat to low and simmer until thickened, about 15 minutes.

Fish Dishes

Spicy Shrimp and Corn Chowder

Serves 6 to 8

Ever since I went to the Boston area, "chowda" has been my preferred pronunciation. I love that word! This chowder is a luscious combination of creamy corn and shrimp with a touch of smoky spice from the chipotle. It's virtually a full meal and would be perfect with a side salad and some crusty bread to soak up the broth. The chipotle is the only obscure ingredient, but it adds a lot of character and is worth seeking out.

PREP

- You can make this entire soup the day before serving, but don't add the cream or the shrimp back in until ready to serve.

OPTIONS

- To reduce heat, discard the chile completely before puréeing.
- You can use frozen corn, although it will be less creamy.
- For a low-fat option, use skim or partially skimmed milk instead of cream. Combine the cold milk with 15 mL (1 tbsp) of cornstarch and add to the soup towards the end, stirring until thickened. If you don't add the cornstarch, the milk will split from the acidity of the wine.

2 tbsp	vegetable oil	*30 mL*
1 lb	medium shrimp, peeled, tail on	*454 g*
2	shallots (or 1 onion), chopped	*2*
1	leek, white part only, finely sliced	*1*
2	cloves garlic, chopped	*2*
1/4 cup	dry white wine	*50 mL*
1	dried chipotle chile, whole (available at specialty shops)	*1*
1	each medium Yukon Gold potato and carrot, peeled and diced	*1*
4	sprigs fresh thyme, stems removed	*4*
1	red pepper, diced	*1*
2	ears fresh corn, kernels removed	*2*
4 cups	fish stock, vegetable stock, or water	*1 L*
1/2 cup	10% cream	*125 mL*
	Salt and pepper, to taste	
	Fresh coriander, chopped (for garnish)	

In large pot, heat oil on high. Add shrimp and sauté for 3 minutes. Remove and reserve. Add shallots and leek and sauté for 4 to 5 minutes, or until soft and golden. Add garlic and toss for 2 to 3 minutes. Add wine and chile and stir to combine. Add potato, carrot, thyme, red pepper, and corn kernels and stir. Add stock and bring to a boil. Cover and reduce heat to low. Simmer for 30 to 35 minutes, or until vegetables are tender and flavour has developed.

Remove chile and discard stem. Purée 1/3 of soup, along with chile, in food processor until smooth. Pour purée in remaining soup mixture and stir to blend. Add cream and simmer, uncovered, for 10 minutes. Add shrimp and cook for 5 minutes. Adjust seasoning. Garnish with coriander.

Thai Shrimp Curry

I have fallen in love with sweet and spicy Thai curries. This is a scaled-down version that doesn't compromise taste and is quick to prepare. Authentic curries are made with customized spice blends, which give them their unique flavours. If you're in a rush, buy a prepared Thai curry paste. The green paste is extremely spicy and the red paste has medium heat. See Options if using prepared curry paste.

1 tbsp	vegetable oil	*15 mL*
1-1/2 lb	large shrimp, peeled and deveined	*681 g*
2	large onions, chopped	*2*
5	shallots, chopped	*5*
3	cloves garlic, chopped	*3*
3	red chiles, finely chopped	*3*
1 tbsp	chopped fresh ginger	*15 mL*
1	small banana, chopped	*1*
1 tsp	turmeric	*5 mL*
1/2 tsp	anise, ground	*2 mL*
1-1/2 tsp	coriander seeds, crushed	*7 mL*
1 tsp	cumin seeds, crushed	*5 mL*
	Salt and pepper, to taste	
1 tsp	grated lime zest	*5 mL*
	Juice of 2 limes	
3	Kaffir lime leaves	*3*
3/4 cup	coconut milk	*175 mL*

Heat oil on high in large pot. Add shrimp and sauté quickly, just until shrimp turn pink. Remove from heat immediately and reserve. To the same pot, add onion and shallots and sauté for several minutes until soft. Add garlic, chile, and ginger and sauté for several minutes. Add banana, spices, and lime zest and juice and stir. Add lime leaves and coconut milk and reduce heat to a simmer. Cover and simmer for 35 to 40 minutes, stirring occasionally. Just before serving, return shrimp to sauce and simmer for 3 minutes, until just heated through. Do not cook shrimp too long.

PREP

- Kaffir lime leaves can be bought at Thai specialty stores, and give the curry its unique flavour. If you are unable to find them fresh, they are sometimes sold dried.

- Curries are perfect when served with a plain white rice like jasmine or basmati.

OPTIONS

- To reduce the fat in this curry, use light coconut milk or reduce coconut milk to 50 mL (1/4 cup) and add 125 mL (1/2 cup) fish stock, clam juice, or chicken stock.

- If using a prepared curry paste, eliminate the chiles and all dried spices. You can also leave out the ginger, since the paste usually contains ginger.

Jasmine Rice Cakes with Sautéed Shrimp and Coconut Banana Sauce

Serves 4

This dish was developed for a show in which I challenged two chefs with a surprise basket of ingredients. I wanted to illustrate that two chefs will use the same ingredients in different ways. I then developed a third recipe with the ingredients. For something totally different, I cooked the rice and formed it into cakes. Then I dipped them in fresh coriander and ginger and pan-fried them lightly. The cakes have a golden spicy crust but the insides stay moist. Served with creamy coconut and banana sauce, this shrimp and rice combo is a unique and delicious entrée.

Rice cakes

1 cup	jasmine rice	*250 mL*
	Freshly cracked black pepper, to taste	
1/2	each small zucchini and yellow pepper, finely diced	*1/2*
1/4 cup	chopped fresh coriander	*50 mL*
1 tbsp	grated fresh ginger	*15 mL*
1/4 cup	vegetable oil	*50 mL*

Shrimp

1 tbsp	butter	*15 mL*
1	onion, chopped	*1*
2 tsp	coarsely grated fresh ginger	*10 mL*
1	Thai chile, minced	*1*
16	large shrimp, tail on, peeled and deveined	*16*
	Zest of 1 lime and juice of 1/2 lime	
1/2 cup	white wine	*125 mL*
1 tbsp	chopped fresh coriander	*15 mL*
	Salt and pepper, to taste	

Sauce

1 tsp	butter	*5 mL*
1	large, ripe banana, sliced	*1*
1/2 cup	coconut milk	*125 mL*
	Juice of 1 lime	

OPTIONS

- You can substitute plain white rice for the jasmine rice. Don't use converted rice; it won't hold together for rice cakes.

- To reduce the fat in the sauce, omit the coconut milk or use a low-fat version.

Cook rice in small pot in 500 mL (2 cups) cold water. Bring to a boil, reduce heat to low, cover, and simmer for 12 minutes. Remove from heat and let stand 5 minutes. Transfer to shallow pan and stir to cool. Season with pepper and add zucchini and yellow pepper. Set aside until completely cool.

While rice is cooking, chop all ingredients for shrimp. Heat butter in large skillet and toss onion, ginger, and chile over high heat. Sauté until onion is soft, about 3 to 4 minutes. Add shrimp and sauté for 1 minute, or until shrimp are just opaque. Add lime zest and juice, white wine, and coriander and adjust seasoning. Remove from heat immediately and set aside.

To prepare sauce, in a small saucepan, brown butter and add banana, coconut milk, and lime juice. Cook over moderate heat for 3 to 5 minutes, or until very thick and creamy. Stir with a fork, mashing banana. Remove from heat and set aside.

Lastly, form rice into 8 round cakes using a little oil on your hands to prevent rice from sticking. Combine coriander and ginger. Dip rice cakes in mixture, coating liberally. Heat oil on high and fry cakes for 2 minutes per side, or until just golden.

Reheat shrimp mixture when rice cakes are ready. Serve 2 rice cakes per plate. Arrange 4 shrimp over rice cakes and drizzle with sauce. Spoon a little banana cream on the side.

PREP

- Although the method in this recipe seems complicated, it's actually quite simple. If the rice cakes seem too ambitious for you, simply flavour the rice as suggested but don't form or fry the cakes.

- A neat way to make perfect rice cakes is to line a jar lid with plastic wrap. Brush with a little oil and mold the rice into it. Remove the plastic and you have a perfect rice cake.

Stir-Fried Shrimp with Orange and Saffron

Serves 4

If I told you that this recipe cooks in about 4 minutes, you'd probably think I was joking. I'll get the timer and you can start peeling the shrimp. You can serve this on its own with some hearty greens if you aren't in a starchy mood. Or, you can serve it with rice or couscous, or toss it with cooked noodles. The taste is bottled sunshine directly from Spain, with a touch of French tarragon.

2 tbsp	olive oil	30 mL
2	cloves garlic, chopped	2
Pinch	saffron threads	Pinch
	Zest of 1 orange	
1/2 lb	medium shrimp, shelled and deveined	227 g
1/4 cup	dry white wine or vermouth	50 mL
	Juice of 1/2 orange	
	Salt and freshly cracked black pepper, to taste	
2 tbsp	chopped fresh tarragon	30 mL

Heat oil in wok or large skillet over high heat for 2 minutes. Add garlic, saffron, and orange zest and stir rapidly. Add shrimp quickly and stir over high heat until cooked, about 3 minutes. Add wine and orange juice, season with salt and pepper, and heat through. Do not cook too long at this point or shrimp will be rubbery. Add tarragon and serve.

PREP

- You should make your accompanying dish before starting the shrimp, since it cooks so quickly.

OPTIONS

- In summer, you can grill the shrimp first, make the sauce separately, and add the shrimp at the end.
- Tarragon can be replaced by chopped parsley, but you will lose the anise flavour.

Latin Rice and Peas with Chorizo and Mussels

This recipe features the intensity of Latin flavours in a full meal that comes together in a flash. The sauce, called a hogo (see It's All Greek to Me!), is a variation on a popular Colombian flavouring liquid. This dish was the crew's favourite from the 1999 season.

Serves 6 to 8

1/2 cup	dried pinto or pigeon beans, or 1 small can (14 oz/398 g)	*125 mL*
2 tbsp	olive oil	*30 mL*
1	large onion, chopped	*1*
1	spicy chorizo sausage, casing removed, chopped	*1*
1/2 tsp	cumin seed, ground	*2 mL*
1/4 tsp	coriander seed, ground	*1 mL*
Pinch	cayenne	*Pinch*
2	cloves garlic, minced	*2*
3	green onions, chopped	*3*
2 cups	chicken stock	*500 mL*
1	large can tomatoes (19 oz/540 g), diced, with juice	*1*
	Salt and freshly cracked black pepper, to taste	
1 cup	long-grain rice	*250 mL*
1 lb	mussels, scrubbed and bearded	*454 g*
2 tbsp	chopped fresh coriander	*30 mL*

Cover dried beans in cold water in small pot. Bring to a boil and simmer 2 minutes. Remove from heat and let soak for 1 hour. Rinse well, cover with cold water, and cook for 20 minutes, or until almost tender.

Meanwhile, in large shallow pot, sauté onion in olive oil on high for 3 minutes, or until soft. Add sausage, cumin, coriander, cayenne, and garlic, reduce heat to medium, and continue to cook until sausage is lightly browned, about 5 minutes. Add green onion, chicken stock, and tomatoes and bring to a boil. Reduce heat to low and simmer for 5 minutes. Adjust seasoning and increase heat to high. Add cooked beans and long-grain rice and stir. Cover and reduce heat to low. Simmer for 15 minutes, then add mussels and coriander. Cover and simmer for 5 minutes, or until mussels open. Remove from heat and let stand several minutes before serving. Adjust seasoning.

PREP

- Finding sources for ethnic ingredients will increase your cooking repertoire. Chorizo can be found at most Latin or ethnic butchers.

- Pigeon or pinto beans can be found in health stores, Latin markets, or bulk stores. You can use red kidney beans if you're in a bind.

- If you're using canned beans, add them at the end with the mussels or they will be mushy.

- This dish can be reheated gently in the microwave, but remove the mussels first.

OPTIONS

- You can replace mussels with shrimp, or omit the seafood altogether.

- Hot Italian sausage can be used instead of chorizo.

Thai Steamed Mussels

Serves 4

If you're in the mood for a great new way to prepare mussels, you'll love this recipe. Having a heaping bowl of mussels for dinner is one of my top 10 things to eat. You can make the whole dish in about 20 minutes. All you need is some crusty bread for dipping and dinner is ready. The aromatic spices, coconut milk, and citrus juices may cause some addiction, so beware.

2 tbsp	vegetable oil	*30 mL*
1	large sweet onion, sliced	*1*
3	cloves garlic, chopped	*3*
1 tbsp	grated fresh ginger	*15 mL*
1	Thai chile, finely chopped	*1*
3	stalks lemongrass, sliced	*3*
1/4 tsp	cumin seed, ground	*1 mL*
	Zest and juice of 1 orange	
	Zest and juice of 1 lime	
1/2 tsp	coriander seed, ground	*2 mL*
1/3 cup	dry white wine	*75 mL*
1/2 cup	coconut milk	*125 mL*
3 lb	PEI mussels, bearded and scrubbed well to remove dirt	*1.4 kg*
1/4 cup	chopped fresh coriander	*50 mL*
	Salt and pepper, to taste	

PREP

- Lemongrass can be purchased at Asian stores and at some grocery stores. It can be frozen for a few weeks if properly wrapped.

- If any mussels are opened before cooking, gently tap them on the counter. If they shut, they are fine. If not, do not use them. Also, don't use mussels that are cracked or broken, since they should be alive before cooking.

OPTION

- If you want a light sauce, leave out the coconut milk and add a little more white wine.

In large deep skillet, heat oil. Add onion and garlic and sauté for 3 minutes. Add ginger, chile, lemongrass, cumin, citrus zest, and coriander seed and sauté for 5 minutes, just to develop flavour. Add wine, coconut milk, juices, and mussels. Cover and steam over medium heat for 5 to 7 minutes, until mussels open. Remove from heat immediately, stir in fresh coriander, and adjust seasoning.

Grilled Halibut Fillet over Arugula with Tomato and Black Olive Salsa, p. 115

Asian Seared Pork Tenderloin with Late Harvest Riesling, **p. 126** (Opposite) Asian Vegetable Stir-Fry with Crispy Bean Threads, **p. 56**

Grilled Beef and Vegetable Pasta, **p. 149** (Opposite) Sautéed King Crab Legs with Citrus Papaya Salsa, **p. 110**

Chicken Breast Scallopini with Chorizo Tomato Sauce, **p. 80** (Opposite) Mediterranean Fish Soup, **p. 112**

Hazelnut Caramel Profiteroles, p. 174

Grilled Lobster with Lemongrass Chive Butter

They'll be knocking down your door once they get a taste of this delicious fusion butter for lobster. The first time I made this dish, people would not let go of the shells. I finally had to say, "Enough!"

Serves 4 to 6

4	whole lobsters (about 1-1/2 lb/681 g each)	4

Lemongrass chive butter

1/3 cup	unsalted butter, melted	75 mL
2	stalks lemongrass, tender part only, finely chopped	2
	Juice of 1/2 lemon	
	Zest of 1 lemon	
2 tbsp	chopped fresh chives	30 mL
	Freshly cracked black pepper, to taste	

Bring at least 5 L (20 cups) water to a boil in large pot. Season well with salt. Cook lobsters for 8 minutes and remove from water immediately. (Cook 2 lobsters at a time to keep water at a boil.) Meanwhile, prepare barbecue by heating on high and brushing grill until very clean. Remove claws and heads from lobster, discarding heads or keeping for stock. Crack claws with hammer or back of heavy knife just until split but with shell still intact. Split tails in half, lengthwise, with sharp heavy knife or shears.

To prepare butter, combine butter and lemongrass in small saucepan on low heat. Simmer gently over very low heat, about 8 to 10 minutes. With a spoon, skim off surface of butter.

Meanwhile, brush flesh side of tails with a little melted butter and place on grill, shell side up, along with claws. Grill for 3 to 5 minutes with lid up. Tails should have grill marks. Remove immediately.

Add lemon juice and zest, chives, and pepper to warm butter just before serving. Serve lobster with warmed butter and plenty of bibs. Don't worry about the mess!

Serve with Grilled Corn and Red Pepper Sauté (see page 59).

PREP

- Always put the live lobster into boiling water, and remove immediately after cooking.

- If you are uncomfortable cooking live lobster, most fish stores have a steaming service. Tell them that you are grilling the lobsters afterwards, so they will undercook them slightly.

- Live lobster should be bought the day of cooking and keeps best wrapped in newspaper in a box in the fridge. If the lobster is not moving when removed from the fridge, it can't be eaten.

OPTION

- To simplify the recipe even more, buy lobster tails, which have more meat and no claws to worry about. You will pay a hefty premium for this convenience. But I love the mess of eating lobster—it's part of the ritual.

Scallops in Creamy Saffron Broth with Spring Vegetables

Serves 4 to 6

This soup, which is really a meal, shows off nature's spring bounty. The only thing you need to serve with this soup is a hearty salad. The flavours are clean and the colour is bright and inviting. Although the recipe calls for many spring vegetables, you can make it in summer and use completely different ones. Allow yourself a little more leeway every time you improvise with a recipe. Pretty soon you'll be so confident that cooking will be a breeze. Should I start writing for Harlequin?

PREP

- Once all vegetables are chopped, this recipe is very simple.
- Scallops should not be overcooked. You introduce their flavour in the beginning by searing them at high heat and then you remove them. They are added back only at the end to heat all the way through. If you are using smaller scallops, reduce the cooking time accordingly.
- You should add vegetables in the order that they will cook. For example, if you use bok choy instead of peas, you will need to add it a little sooner to ensure it cooks through.

1 tbsp	butter	*15 mL*
12	medium scallops, fresh or frozen	*12*
	Salt and freshly cracked black pepper, to taste	
2	large shallots, finely chopped	*2*
1/2 tsp	grated fresh ginger	*2 mL*
1	clove garlic, chopped	*1*
2 cups	fish stock (or clam juice)	*500 mL*
1/2 cup	dry white wine or vermouth	*125 mL*
	Juice and grated zest of 1 lime	
Pinch	saffron	*Pinch*
8	baby red new potatoes, cut in half and washed	*8*
8	spears asparagus, trimmed and cut into thirds	*8*
1 tsp	cornstarch	*5 mL*
1 tbsp	water	*15 mL*
1/3 cup	35% cream	*75 mL*
1/2 cup	fresh peas	*125 mL*
	Assorted fresh herbs (chives, parsley, and chervil), chopped (for garnish)	

Herb oil (optional)

1	bunch fresh chives	*1*
1/4 cup	fresh parsley	*50 mL*
1/4 cup	olive oil	*50 mL*

In medium sauté pan, heat butter on high. Season scallops with salt and pepper and sear for 2 to 3 minutes per side, or until golden. Remove immediately and reserve. To same pan, add shallots, ginger, and garlic and reduce heat to medium. Sauté for 3 to 5 minutes, or until soft. Add stock, wine, lime zest and juice, and saffron and bring to a boil. Add potatoes, reduce heat to low, and allow liquid to reduce by 1/3. Check potatoes after 8 minutes. If they are tender, remove from liquid, reserve, and continue to reduce stock. Meanwhile, blanch asparagus.

In small bowl, combine cornstarch and water. Add cream and stir to combine. Add to broth mixture. Continue to simmer until reduced by 1/3, about 6 to 8 minutes. Just before serving, add scallops, asparagus, peas, potatoes, and herbs. Simmer for 2 to 3 minutes to warm through. Adjust seasoning.

To prepare herb oil, if desired, combine all ingredients in food processor. Pulse until finely chopped and strain through cheesecloth.

Serve 3 scallops per person and drizzle with sauce and vegetables. For added flavour, drizzle with a little herb oil.

OPTIONS

- The cream is not essential to this dish, as there is plenty of great flavour without it.
- The herb oil will give you extra presentation points, as it provides a bright green drizzle through the creamy broth.

Grilled Calamari with Lemon Olive Oil Marinade

Serves 4

This is a great summertime grill item. Squid is very easy to cook because it only takes 2 to 3 minutes. Since the bodies are a little tricky to clean, you can buy them already cleaned, frozen or fresh. The grill should be very hot and, once cooked, the calamari should be dropped into the marinade to soak up the flavours of lemon and olive oil.

1-1/2 lb	small calamari	*681 g*
1/4 cup	olive oil	*50 mL*
	Juice of 1 lemon	
1 tsp	dried oregano	*5 mL*
	Salt and freshly cracked black pepper, to taste	

Clean squid by removing head from body and cutting the tentacles above the eyes.

Remove the soft bone from body and rinse thoroughly. Peel skin from the side flaps of squid and trim. Meanwhile, heat grill until very hot and oil well to prevent sticking.

Brush squid very lightly with oil. Grill for 2 to 3 minutes on each side, or until tender. Do not overcook. Slice into rings. Combine olive oil, lemon juice, oregano, salt, and pepper and toss warm squid into mixture.

PREP

- Be sure to choose the smaller squid, which is more tender.
- Squid either should be cooked for a very short while (2 to 3 minutes per side) or should be braised for 35 to 40 minutes to lose the chewy bite it develops.

OPTION

- Add a splash of balsamic vinegar for a deeper, tangy flavour.

Sautéed Calamari with Black Olives and Pine Nuts

Serves 4 to 6
as an appetizer

Don't be afraid of calamari. It's only squid and is enjoyed in every country along the Mediterranean. This is one of my absolute favourite ways to prepare it. It's not deep-fried and therefore is much lower in fat, but the flavour jumps off the plate. The combination of olives, mushrooms, and herbs makes a perfect appetizer for the middle of the table while pasta is boiling away on the stove.

6	small squid, cleaned (about 3/4 lb/341 g) 6
	Salt and pepper, to taste
	Flour (for dredging)
3 tbsp	olive oil *45 mL*
3	large oyster mushrooms, torn gently by hand *3*
1	small onion, sliced *1*
2	cloves garlic, chopped *2*
1/4 cup	black olives, pitted and sliced *50 mL*
2	plum tomatoes, finely diced *2*
1 tsp	dried oregano *5 mL*
1/4 cup	chopped fresh parsley *50 mL*
2 tbsp	toasted pine nuts *30 mL*
	Lemon wedges (for garnish)

PREP

• This dish can also be a main course when served with steamed greens and a tomato salad.

• For tips on preparing the squid, see prep notes in Grilled Calamari with Lemon Olive Oil Marinade (see page 108).

• You can save leftover squid and serve at room temperature the next day. Make sure you keep covered in the fridge overnight.

OPTIONS

• You can use Portobello or shiitake mushrooms if you can't find oyster.

• You can leave out the flour, but the squid will have less body.

Frozen squid can be used if they are cleaned and ready to cook. If using fresh squid, make sure you remove ink sack and head and discard innards. Turn bodies inside out and rinse thoroughly. Slice bodies into thin rings and leave tentacles whole. Rinse well and pat dry. Season with salt and pepper. Dredge in flour.

Meanwhile, in a large skillet heat 30 mL (2 tbsp) olive oil on high. When oil is starting to smoke, add squid and toss vigorously until golden, about 2 minutes. Remove from heat immediately and set aside.

In same pan, heat remaining olive oil until hot. Add oyster mushrooms and toss. Add onion and sauté for 1 minute. Add garlic, olives, tomatoes, and oregano. Sprinkle with parsley and pine nuts and return squid to pan. Toss several times and adjust seasoning. Serve with lemon wedges.

Sautéed King Crab Legs with Citrus Papaya Salsa

Serves 4

This recipe is an absolute treat. King crab legs are my favourite seafood—even more succulent than lobster. This was my version of a chef's challenge, in which we all came up with recipes out of a basket of ingredients. Technically this dish is an appetizer, but it's such a big hitter that I had to put it in the seafood category. King crab is simple to prepare because it comes steamed and frozen. All you have to do is figure out how you want to serve it and, since this recipe is already waiting, a lot of your work is done.

1	carrot, sliced lengthwise, very thinly (use a mandolin)	*1*
2	frozen king crab legs, thawed	*2*
1 tbsp	butter	*15 mL*
2	medium carrots, julienned	*2*
1	leek, white part only, julienned	*1*
	Zest of 1 orange, grated	
	Salt and freshly cracked black pepper, to taste	
	Juice of 1/2 lime	
1/4 cup	chopped fresh parsley	*50 mL*
	Orange slices (for garnish)	
	Lime wedges (for garnish)	

Salsa

1	ripe papaya, peeled and seeded, diced	*1*
1	sweet onion, finely diced	*1*
2	green onions, finely chopped	*2*
	Several drops Tabasco sauce	
1	navel orange, segmented and cut into small cubes	*1*

PREP

• Unless you live in Alaska, you will probably be buying frozen, steamed king crab legs. It's easier to work with crab legs when they are not completely thawed because the meat comes out easily.

• Crab legs are also perfect for throwing on the barbecue. Again, ensure you make a few slits in the legs, grill for a couple of minutes on all sides, and let everyone dig in.

Combine all ingredients for salsa, except orange segments, in medium bowl. Toss to blend. Remove 1/3 of mixture and pulse in food processor until smooth. Return to bowl of remaining salsa, add orange segments, and toss. Cover and reserve until ready to use. Can be made the day before.

Immerse four thin slices of carrot in ice water. They will begin to curl after about 15 minutes.

Snip lengthwise down both sides of crab legs with shears and remove meat. Reserve shells for soup or sauces, if desired. They can be frozen.

In large sauté pan, melt butter on high. Add julienned carrot, leek, and orange zest. Toss until just soft. Add crab and sauté for 1 to 2 minutes, or until just warmed through. Season with salt and pepper, add lime juice, and sprinkle with parsley.

To assemble, lay 1 carrot spiral in the middle of each plate. Place 1/4 of crab mixture in each spiral, creating a loose spring roll. Spoon a little salsa over top and garnish with orange slices and lime wedges.

OPTIONS

- These flavours also work well with scallops or lobster.
- For a dramatic presentation, save the pincers on the crab legs and arrange two on each plate.
- Leftovers can be sprinkled at room temperature over a bed of greens and served as a salad.

Mediterranean Fish Soup

Serves 4 to 6

This is my version of a French bouillabaisse, a classical fish soup. Since most of the fish traditionally used in this soup are not native to our waters I thought I'd give you my version, which is North America–friendly. Monkfish, known as poor man's lobster, has great texture and is perfect in soups such as this because it can be simmered without falling apart.

1/4 cup	olive oil	*50 mL*
1/2 lb	monkfish, cubed	*227 g*
	Salt and pepper, to taste	
1	medium onion, chopped	*1*
1	clove garlic, chopped	*1*
1	bulb fresh fennel, chopped	*1*
1/2 cup	dry white wine	*125 mL*
	Zest of 1 orange and 1 lemon	
Pinch	saffron	*Pinch*
4 cups	fish stock	*1 L*
	Juice of 1/2 lemon	
2	Italian tomatoes, chopped	*2*
1 lb	mussels, washed and bearded	*454 g*
	Fresh parsley, chopped, to taste	

PREP

- This should be a very rustic soup, so simply chop all the vegetables roughly to save you time.
- This soup reheats very nicely, but remove the mussels before reheating, as they will become rubbery if cooked too long.

OPTION

- The fennel can be omitted if you don't like the mild anise flavour.

In large pot, heat 1/2 the olive oil on medium. Add monkfish and sauté gently for 2 minutes, or until lightly golden. Sprinkle with salt and pepper. Remove from heat and remove fish and reserve. Add remaining oil, onion, and garlic and stir until translucent, about 3 minutes. Add fennel, wine, zest, and saffron and continue to simmer while stirring occasionally for about 4 minutes. Add stock and lemon juice. Simmer for 20 minutes, or until flavours develop and fennel is tender.

Just before serving, bring soup back to a boil. Add tomatoes and fish and adjust seasoning. Simmer on medium until fish is tender, about 6 to 8 minutes. Add mussels, cover, and continue to simmer until they open, about 3 to 5 minutes. Remove immediately and sprinkle with parsley. Serve with lots of bread, if desired.

Cornmeal-Crusted Fillet of Sea Bass

This recipe may be the easiest and most tempting I've ever made. Sea bass is a very durable fish with a meaty quality. Dredging it in cornmeal gives it a golden colour and a crisp crust. The coulis is a fresh-tasting raw sauce that wakes the taste buds.

1/2 cup	cornmeal	125 mL
1/4 cup	chopped fresh parsley	50 mL
1/2 tsp	coriander seeds, cracked	2 mL
4	pieces of sea bass fillet (about 6 oz/170 g each)	4
	Salt and freshly cracked black pepper, to taste	
	Olive oil (for searing fish)	

Lime tomato coulis

3	medium roma tomatoes, roughly chopped	3
1	small red onion, finely diced	1
1/2 tsp	finely chopped jalapeño chile (optional)	2 mL
	Juice of 1 lime	
2 tbsp	extra virgin olive oil	30 mL
1/2 tsp	honey	2 mL
	Zest of 1 lime	
1 tbsp	chopped fresh coriander	15 mL
	Salt and pepper, to taste	

In shallow baking dish or pan, combine cornmeal, parsley, and coriander seeds. Toss well. Season fish with salt and pepper and dredge in cornmeal mixture, coating well. Transfer to clean pan and refrigerate until ready to cook. Preheat oven to 190°C (375°F).

To prepare coulis, combine tomatoes, onion, chile (if using), lime juice, olive oil, and honey in food processor and pulse until puréed. Strain into medium bowl. Add lime zest and coriander and whisk until well combined. Adjust seasoning. Set aside.

In large skillet, heat olive oil on high. Sear sea bass 2 minutes on each side, or until golden. Transfer to roasting pan or baking sheet and bake for 8 to 10 minutes, depending on thickness of fish, until firm. Remove from oven and serve immediately with coulis. Sauce will have separated, so whisk again just before serving.

Serves 4

PREP

- The coulis is very simple to make but separates quickly. Just whisk or pulse a few times in the blender to get back its smooth consistency.
- You can rub the fish with a little olive oil so cornmeal sticks to flesh more easily.

OPTION

- Substitute halibut or salmon if you can't get sea bass.

Pan-Fried Rainbow Trout with Dill and Dijon

Serves 4

I really want to encourage you to try whole rainbow trout if you have not yet done so. It is quick, easy to find, and delicious. Two fish will feed four people and will take about 15 minutes to cook in total. The simple addition of lots of fresh herbs, mustard, and lemon brings out the best character in the fish. I love to serve this fish on a bed of nappa and carrot slaw (see page 17).

2	medium whole rainbow trout, cleaned	2
1/4 cup	chopped fresh dill	50 mL
1/4 cup	chopped fresh parsley	50 mL
1/2	jalapeño chile, chopped	1/2
2 tbsp	Dijon mustard	30 mL
	Juice and zest of 2 lemons	
	Salt and freshly cracked black pepper, to taste	
	Flour (for dredging)	
2 tbsp	olive oil	30 mL
2 tbsp	vegetable oil	30 mL

Preheat oven to 180°C (350°F).

Rub cavity and outside of fish with herbs, jalapeño, mustard, and lemon zest. Season with salt and pepper. Dredge lightly in flour.

Heat oils in large frying pan on high heat. Fry fish for 5 minutes per side, or until golden. Finish cooking fish in oven for 6 to 8 minutes, or until flesh is still firm but meat comes away from bone. Remove from oven and squeeze lemon juice over top.

PREP

- The key to success with this recipe is to buy very fresh trout. Ensure that the fish has a delicate aroma and that its flesh is firm, eyes are not sunken, and gills are bright.
- The scales on the fish are very delicate, so they don't need to be removed before cooking.

OPTIONS

- You can grill this fish in the summer, but don't dredge it in flour first. When grilling whole small fish, avoid turning them more than once. Lift the head up gently to see if skin is browned and then turn it over. To guarantee that inside is cooked, reduce heat to low and close the barbecue cover for the last 5 minutes. Once removed from the grill, the fish will continue to cook for a couple of minutes.
- Omit the jalapeño if you don't like it spicy.

Grilled Halibut Fillet over Arugula with Tomato and Black Olive Salsa

This recipe became my signature dish from the moment I first made it. I really wanted to show how easy it is to create a restaurant-style dish in about 20 minutes, right in your very own kitchen. My producer was amazed at how quickly it comes together and how sophisticated it looks with minimal effort. It's a recipe that will become a favourite.

Serves 4

4-6 oz	halibut fillets	*114-170 g*
3 tbsp	olive oil	*45 mL*
	Salt and freshly cracked black pepper, to taste	
2	sprigs fresh thyme	*2*
1/4 cup	chopped fresh coriander	*50 mL*
1	yellow pepper, diced	*1*
1	red pepper, diced	*1*
4	plum tomatoes, diced	*4*
1/3 cup	chopped pitted kalamata olives	*75 mL*
1	green onion, finely chopped	*1*
1	bunch arugula, trimmed and washed thoroughly	*1*

Rub fish with 15 mL (1 tbsp) olive oil. Season with salt and pepper and sprinkle with thyme and 1/4 of coriander. Grill fish on well-heated grill or grill pan for 4 minutes per side, or until done to your liking.

Meanwhile, heat remaining oil in medium saucepan. Over medium heat, sauté peppers and tomatoes until just soft, about 3 to 5 minutes. Remove from heat. Add olives, green onion, and remaining coriander. Season with pepper.

To serve, place arugula on plate, top with fish, and drizzle with salsa.

PREP
- There is so little preparation of any type for this dish that you can simply serve it with some easy potatoes for a full meal.

OPTIONS
- If you can't get arugula, use spinach or hearty greens.
- You can replace halibut with sea bass or swordfish.

Steamed Halibut in Banana Leaf with Warm Spicy Oil

Serves 4

PREP

- Since the oil loses its punch when heated too intensely, warm it gently to slowly draw flavour from the garlic and chile. Everyone will ask you where you got it.

- To test if fish is cooked, insert a small knife into its centre. If cooked, the knife will be just warm. Remove the fish immediately, as it will continue to cook from residual heat.

- Don't start steaming fish until vegetables or starch is ready.

OPTIONS

- Many other fish can be steamed using this method, including sea bass, salmon, red snapper, and pickerel. Ask your fishmonger for suggestions.

- Banana leaves can be found at Latin stores in the freezer section. If you can't find them, wrap the fish in parchment paper, or even in plastic wrap, and steam the same way.

Using banana leaves is a beautiful way to portion the fish and steam it with maximum flavour. If you don't have a bamboo steamer, which is very inexpensive and easy to find, you can steam the fish in a double boiler or vegetable steamer. The spicy oil is added at the end so everyone can control the amount of fat and extra zip. This dish is ideal for those of you who are working out and looking for the perfect balance of fat, protein, and carbohydrates; it has no cholesterol, except what's in the fish. Serve it with half a baked sweet potato and some steamed greens.

4	halibut fillets (each about 6 oz/170 g)	*4*
	Salt and freshly cracked black pepper, to taste	
1	banana leaf, cut into 4 squares, each 10 x 10-in/25 x 25-cm	*1*
2	cloves garlic, minced	*2*
1 tsp	cumin seeds, toasted and ground	*5 mL*
4	Kaffir lime leaves, or grated zest of 2 limes	*4*
4	pieces butcher's twine, each 12 in/30 cm	*4*

Spicy oil

1/4 cup	extra virgin olive oil	*50 mL*
1	clove garlic, finely sliced	*1*
1 tsp	chopped fresh coriander	*5 mL*
1/2	jalapeño chile, sliced into rings, seeds intact	*1/2*
	Juice of 1/2 lime	

Prepare bamboo steamer or double boiler with perforated insert. Fill bottom with water and bring to boil. Reduce heat to low and simmer. Cover until ready to use.

Meanwhile, season fish with salt and pepper on both sides. Lay banana leaves out. Place a fillet on the middle of each. Sprinkle with garlic, cumin, and pepper. Top each with 1 lime leaf. Wrap banana leaf around fish like parcel and tie with butcher's twine.

Place ingredients for oil in small saucepan and warm gently on low heat until fish is ready. Do not heat rapidly! Strain before serving.

Steam fish for 7 to 8 minutes, or until centre of fish is warm (see Prep). Remove from steamer immediately and serve with warm oil.

Salmon with Light White Wine Sabayon

When you feel like a slick-looking main course that is very simple to make and has a French twist, this salmon will oblige. Everyone will be so thankful because they'll think that you spent hours preparing it, when you actually whipped it together in minutes. Imagine the bonus points you'll get. The pale pink salmon and creamy yellow sauce are a perfect partner for Lemon Rosemary Green Beans (see page 60)

4	pieces of salmon fillet (each 3 oz/85 g) *4*
	Salt and pepper, to taste
1 tsp	vegetable oil *5 mL*
	Zest of 1 lemon
	Zest of 1 lime

Sabayon

3	egg yolks *3*
1/2 cup	white wine *125 mL*
	Juice of 1/2 lemon
	Salt and pepper, to taste
1 tbsp	chopped fresh chives *15 mL*

Preheat broiler to 230°C (450°F). Sprinkle salmon lightly with salt and pepper, brush very lightly with vegetable oil, then brush with lemon and lime zest. Place fillets in broiling pan and cook under broiler until just golden, about 4 minutes on each side.

Meanwhile, combine all ingredients for sabayon, except chives, in medium stainless steel bowl. Whisk vigorously over double boiler until thick and creamy, about 3 to 5 minutes. Sprinkle with chives. Serve with salmon.

PREP

- To make a great sabayon, you need a sturdy pot with about 5 cm (2 in) of water in the bottom. The bowl that sits on top should be stainless steel and should not touch the surface of the water. The water should be simmering very gently, not boiling. Start making the sabayon about 3 minutes before you take the salmon out of oven and whisk vigorously so egg yolks don't scramble.

OPTION

- If you are watching your yolk intake or don't want a creamy sauce, blend 3 tbsp extra virgin olive oil with the juice and zest of 1/2 lemon and 1 tsp Dijon mustard. Add the pepper and chives at the end.

Pan-Seared Atlantic Salmon with Wilted Spinach

Serves 4 to 6

I developed this recipe with a Caesar theme (the drink, not the salad). The zesty flavours of the vodka and clamato juice are delicious with seared salmon. Finally, the whole thing is laid on a bed of wilted spinach, which is the perfect contrast to the salmon. Don't worry about prep time because this dish takes about 20 minutes in total and the entire meal is made in the same skillet. If you want easy, this is it!

PREP

- You can buy tail pieces of salmon fillet about 20 to 25 cm (8 to 10 in) long and slice them on a bias into thin slices. Or, a good fishmonger will be able to do this for you. Start from the tail end and follow the slope of the tail to achieve the bias.

- Once this dish is cooked, you don't want to warm it for too long or it will dry out. It can be served at room temperature with the warm sauce over top.

- This is an ideal recipe to serve two people. Simply divide the recipe in half.

- Grape tomatoes are a specialty variety that is shaped like a grape and is very sweet. You can use cherry tomatoes instead.

Salmon

8	3-oz/85-g pieces salmon fillet, cut diagonally (1/2-3/4 in/1-2 cm thick) 8
	Salt and freshly cracked black pepper, to taste
2 tbsp	each chopped fresh dill and olive oil 30 mL

Spinach

1 tbsp	olive oil or butter 15 mL
1	large bunch spinach, leaves only, washed and chopped 1
2	green onions, sliced diagonally 2
Pinch	nutmeg Pinch
	Salt and freshly cracked black pepper, to taste

Sauce

2 tsp	olive oil 10 mL
2	shallots, very finely diced 2
1	stalk celery, finely diced 1
1/2 cup	clamato juice 125 mL
1 tbsp	vodka (optional) 15 mL
	Several drops Tabasco sauce
2 tsp	lemon juice 10 mL
1	vine-ripened tomato, cored and diced 1
	Salt and freshly cracked black pepper, to taste
	chives, finely chopped (for garnish) 4
8	cherry or grape tomatoes, cut in half (for garnish) 8

Chop all ingredients before beginning to cook, as cooking process is very quick.

Season salmon with salt and pepper and sprinkle with dill. Heat olive oil on high in large skillet. Sear salmon, working with 4 pieces at a time, about 2 minutes per side, or until golden on both sides. Remove and set aside, covering to keep warm.

To cook spinach, return pan to heat on high and add 1/2 the oil or butter. When golden, add 1/2 the spinach and 1/2 the green onions and toss quickly until just wilted. Add nutmeg and season to taste. Remove spinach and set aside with salmon. Repeat with other half of ingredients.

To make sauce, heat oil in same pan. Add shallots and celery, sautéing until soft, about 3 minutes. Add remaining ingredients and cook over medium high heat until slightly thickened.

Arrange salmon with spinach on plates and drizzle sauce over top. Sprinkle with chives and cherry tomatoes for garnish.

OPTIONS

- You can use only olive oil instead of butter.
- To save you time washing spinach, try using prepackaged and washed baby spinach. It will literally take 1 minute to wilt in the pan.

Grilled Salmon with Citrus Salsa

Serves 4

This is a very fresh, light recipe for salmon fillets. The contrast of the salmon with all the citrus juices and zest results in a lean preparation whose only fat source comes from the salmon. However, the fat in salmon is Omega 3 fatty acid, which is essential to the body.

1	medium red onion, finely diced	*1*
1	mango, peeled and diced	*1*
1	red pepper, diced	*1*
	Juice and grated zest of 1 lime	
	Juice and grated zest of 1/2 lemon	
	Juice and grated zest of 1 orange	
1 tbsp	chopped fresh coriander	*15 mL*
1 tbsp	chopped fresh chives	*15 mL*
1/2	small chile pepper, finely chopped	*1/2*
1/2 tsp	salt	*2 mL*
4	pieces salmon fillet (each 6 oz/170 g)	*4*
1 tsp	vegetable oil	*5 mL*

PREP

- When grilling fish, you need to properly season your grill. That doesn't mean adding salt and pepper, but it does mean rubbing with neutral oil and heating for about 10 minutes to burn off any residue that will cause the fish to stick. Just before grilling you can go over your grill with a good-quality brush.

OPTIONS

- You can simplify the salsa by omitting the mango.
- I would probably only substitute swordfish or a similar meaty or rich-tasting fish. A delicate fish like red snapper will not hold up well to the sugar and spice of the salsa.

Combine all ingredients, except salmon and oil, in a bowl and set aside. Cover and let stand in the refrigerator until ready to use.

Preheat grill at high. Sprinkle salmon fillets lightly with salt and pepper and brush very lightly with oil. Grill salmon for 4 minutes on each side, or until golden and just firm.

Red Snapper Bundles in Phyllo

This is an elegant way to serve fish, where each person is served a neat, crispy phyllo bundle. The cream sauce is divine but can be eliminated if you're not in the mood for a rich, creamy sauce.

Serves 4

2 tbsp	olive oil	*30 mL*
4	medium shallots, chopped	*4*
1 tbsp	chopped fresh dill	*15 mL*
4	red snapper fillets (each about 6 oz/170 g)	*4*
	Salt and pepper, to taste	
	Juice of 1/2 lime	
8	sheets phyllo pastry, thawed	*8*
1/4 cup	melted butter (for phyllo)	*50 mL*

Sauce (optional)

1/2 cup	dry white wine	*125 mL*
2	shallots, finely chopped	*2*
1 cup	fish stock	*250 mL*
1/2 cup	35% cream	*125 mL*
Pinch	saffron	*Pinch*
	Salt and cracked black pepper, to taste	
	Fresh chives, chopped, to taste (optional)	

Preheat oven to 190°C (375°F).

In small frying pan, heat oil, add shallots, and sauté until soft, about 3 minutes. Remove from heat and add dill. Set aside.

Season fish with salt and pepper and squeeze a little lime juice on top of each fillet. Brush 2 phyllo leaves at a time with butter and place on top of each other. Place phyllo with shorter side in front of you. Lay 1 piece of fish in middle of bottom third of each prepared phyllo. Spread 1/4 of shallot mixture over each piece of fish. Fold edges into middle and fold over, away from you, until fish is fully wrapped. Lay bundles, seam side down, on baking sheet and pierce the tops several times to allow steam to escape. *(continues)*

PREP

- Red snapper is a delicious fish, but it is a little difficult to fillet. Ask your fishmonger to fillet it and remove the little pin bones that run down its sides. Leave the skin on the fish.

- Phyllo can be purchased at most upscale grocers, but it has a quicker turnaround in Greek stores. Defrost it in the fridge for several hours. I always recommend buying two packages, since you can never tell if it's torn to shreds until you actually open it. It eliminates a lot of frustration.

OPTIONS

- The sauce is quite rich; you can easily serve this fish with a squeeze of fresh lime juice.

- Look for white, firm fish as alternatives to the snapper; pompano, sole, and halibut will work. Be sure to adjust the cooking time, depending on how thick the fillet is.

Bake on middle rack of oven until crispy and golden, about 18 to 20 minutes. To test if fish is done, pierce middle of fish with sharp knife. When knife is removed, it should feel just warm to the touch.

To prepare sauce, combine white wine, shallots, fish stock, cream, and saffron in small saucepan. Bring to a boil and reduce heat to low. Simmer, uncovered, until reduced by half, about 10 minutes. Season with salt and pepper and add chives, if desired. Serve over fish.

Jerked Swordfish Skewers with Red Lentils

Serves 4 to 6

PREP

- It is best to start with the spice rub. There is a bit of acidity in the blend, as well as a ton of chile, so it keeps well in the fridge for a couple of weeks if covered.

- Use extreme caution when handling the scotch bonnets, as they are very hot. Do not touch your eyes unless you wash your hands thoroughly. It's good practice to use latex gloves when chopping chiles. If you get a dose of heat, the best thing to do is eat a piece of bread to absorb it. To reduce the heat, remove the seeds and ribbing of chile.

This recipe was inspired by my many trips to Jamaica. The traditional jerk is made with pork or chicken and is a spit-cooking method that is absolutely delicious but time consuming. Once you use this method on a dish, it is called "jerked" not "jerk." The very spicy and sweet notes add interest to the swordfish. I'm serving it with red lentils to give you a taste of India. Also, consider Pan-Fried Plantain (see page 46) as a side dish.

Spice rub

1	bunch fresh thyme, leaves only, chopped	*1*
2	sprigs fresh coriander, chopped	*2*
1/2	bunch green onions, chopped	*1/2*
1 tbsp	chopped fresh ginger	*15 mL*
2	cloves garlic, chopped	*2*
	Juice of 2 limes	
2 tbsp	white wine vinegar	*30 mL*
1-2	large scotch bonnet chiles, stemmed and chopped	*1-2*
3/4 tsp	ground allspice	*3 mL*
1/2 tsp	ground cinnamon	*2 mL*
1 tsp	freshly cracked pepper	*5 mL*
3 tbsp	olive oil	*45 mL*

Combine all ingredients in food processor and pulse until smooth. Store in covered container in fridge until ready to use. Will keep for a couple of weeks.

Swordfish

1-1/2 lb	swordfish, cut into 1/2-in/1-cm strips	681 g
1 tsp	vegetable oil	5 mL
1	small onion, chopped	1
1	clove garlic, chopped	1
1-1/4 cup	water	300 mL
	Salt, to taste	
1	small cinnamon stick	1
1 cup	red lentils, rinsed	250 mL
	Vegetable oil (for brushing grill or grill pan)	
	Fresh lime slices (for garnish)	

Soak wooden or bamboo skewers in water for 20 minutes while preparing spice rub.

Rub swordfish with spice mix. Thread swordfish strips onto skewers.

In medium saucepan, heat oil. Sauté onion and garlic until soft, about 3 to 4 minutes. Add water, salt, and cinnamon stick and bring to a boil. Add lentils and reduce heat to low. Simmer, uncovered, for 10 to 12 minutes, or until lentils are tender and water is absorbed. Remove cinnamon stick.

Meanwhile, preheat barbecue or grill pan on high heat and brush with oil. Season skewers with salt and cook for 2 minutes on each side. Fish should be moist. Thread a slice of lime on each skewer.

Serve fish skewers on top of lentils, with some pan-fried plantain, if desired.

Grilled Swordfish
with Grilled Fennel Persillade

Serves 4

Swordfish is probably the meatiest-tasting fish you'll encounter, so I thought I'd give it something with meaty flavour to spar with. My version of a French persillade is quite unique. Traditionally, a persillade is a combination of garlic and parsley that is added to a dish just before the end of cooking. I had to make some changes, of course, and add some grilled fennel and capers, among other things, to give you a type of salsa that is spooned onto the fish after cooking.

4	pieces swordfish (each about 6 oz/170 g)	*4*
1/4 cup	chopped mixed herbs	*50 mL*
2 tbsp	olive oil	*30 mL*
	Zest of 2 lemons, grated	
	Salt and freshly cracked black pepper, to taste	

Persillade

3	green onions, chopped	*3*
1	clove garlic, minced	*1*
1/4 cup	extra virgin olive oil	*50 mL*
2 tbsp	white wine vinegar	*30 mL*
	Juice of 1/2 lemon and zest of 1 lemon, grated	
12	capers	*12*
1/4 cup	chopped parsley	*50 mL*
	Freshly cracked black pepper, to taste	
1/2	bulb fennel, grilled and chopped	*1/2*

PREP

• Leftover fish can be broken up, tossed with remaining persillade, and served at room temperature as a salad.

OPTIONS

• You can combine all persillade ingredients in a food processor without the fennel and brush it on the fish just before it is finished grilling. Grill the fennel separately and you have a bit of a twist.

• You can use fresh tuna instead of swordfish, but don't substitute a delicate fish because the other flavours are too strong.

Combine all ingredients for persillade, except fennel, in medium bowl and stir. Remove 1/3 of mixture and pulse several times in food processor to chop finely. Add back to mixture and adjust seasoning. Add fennel and set aside until ready to use.

Rub herbs, olive oil, and lemon zest on fish and season with salt and pepper. Preheat grill on high. Grill for 4 minutes per side, or until done to liking. Serve with persillade.

The Meat's the Thing

Asian Seared Pork Tenderloin with Late Harvest Riesling

Serves 4

This fusion recipe was inspired by a trip to a Niagara winery. Since pork and apples are made for each other, I have gone a step further and combined the pork with a late harvest wine that has apple aromas. I then added a little soy sauce, some ginger, and some fresh grapes to the sauce, creating this simple dish where Asia meets the Niagara escarpment.

2	pork tenderloins (about 3/4 lb/341 g each)	2
1 tsp	vegetable oil	5 mL

Glaze

1/2 tsp	chile oil	2 mL
1 tbsp	tamarind paste	15 mL
1 tbsp	soy sauce	15 mL
1 tbsp	grated fresh ginger	15 mL
1	clove garlic, minced	1

Sauce

1 tsp	vegetable oil	5 mL
1	clove garlic, minced	1
1 tsp	finely chopped fresh ginger	5 mL
1 cup	late harvest Vidal or Riesling	250 mL
1 cup	chicken stock	250 mL
2 tsp	apple butter	10 mL
1 tsp	cornstarch	5 mL
1 tbsp	cold water	15 mL
1/2 cup	seedless green grapes	125 mL
	Juice of 1/2 lime (optional)	

PREP

- The pork tenderloin should not be cooked too long or it will dry out. Count on 15 minutes at 190°C (375°F). When you press the meat with tongs, it should give a little and should not feel very tight. For a precise temperature check, insert a meat thermometer into meat before cooking. When it reads 70°C (160°F), you should remove the meat from the oven.

- This entire dish will take about 30 minutes to prepare, including the cooking time because while the pork is cooking you can work on the sauce. Plan to put the rice on when you put the tenderloin in the oven to roast for the best timing.

Preheat oven to 190°C (375°F).

Combine chile oil with tamarind paste, soy sauce, ginger, and garlic in food processor until smooth. Brush mixture over pork.

Heat large skillet on medium and add vegetable oil. When pan is hot, add pork and sear well on all sides, about 3 minutes. Remove from heat, transfer pork to roasting pan, and finish cooking in oven for 15 minutes, or until done to your liking but still juicy. (It should not be dry, like at those Sunday dinners we all remember.)

Meanwhile, to make sauce, return pan that pork was seared in to medium heat. Add oil, garlic, and ginger and sauté for 3 minutes. Add Riesling, chicken stock, and apple butter and reduce for 5 minutes, or until slightly thickened. Mix cornstarch and water. Add grapes and cornstarch mixture to pan. Bring to a boil while stirring over medium heat. Remove from heat. Taste sauce and add lime juice, if desired.

Slice pork and serve with sauce and jasmine rice.

OPTIONS
- You certainly could use these same flavours for pork chops; simply adjust the cooking time in the oven.
- A dry Riesling could be used for a sauce that is more tangy.
- You could also slice the tenderloin thinly and stir-fry it instead of roasting.

Pork Loin Chops Stuffed with Dates

I was inspired to develop this recipe after visiting an incredible date farm in California. Dates are a great source of iron and I wanted to illustrate that their use should not be restricted to desserts. Here, you will experience a burst of citrus and tangy flavours that are mellowed by the sweet meaty texture of the date. Finally, this recipe is in keeping with my simple theme, as it takes about 30 minutes to prepare.

Serves 4

4	pork loin chops, boneless, butterflied	4
2	cloves garlic, minced	2
1 tsp	chopped fresh ginger	5 mL
	Zest of 1 lime, grated	
	Salt and pepper, to taste	
1/3 cup	fresh parsley, chopped	75 mL
2	large dates, pits removed, chopped (about 2 tbsp/30 mL)	2
1/8 tsp	chile flakes or chopped fresh jalapeño	0.5 mL
4 tsp	sesame seeds	20 mL
1 tbsp	vegetable oil	15 mL

PREP
- To butterfly chops, cut horizontally through the middle of chops, but not all the way, leaving the end intact. Open the halves and you have a butterfly shape.

- Regular molasses has
a completely different
flavour to that of
pomegranate molasses,
so you should expect
a sweeter taste if
substituting. I would add
a little more lime juice
to balance the sugar.

Sauce

	Juice of 1/2 lime	
1 tbsp	dark rum	15 mL
2 tbsp	pomegranate molasses	30 mL
1 cup	chicken stock	250 mL
1 tbsp	coriander (optional, for garnish)	15 mL

Preheat oven to 190°C (375°F).

Arrange pork chops on cutting board, opening both sides to lay flat. Pound each side until about 1 cm (1/2 in) thick. Sprinkle one side with 1/2 of garlic and ginger. Sprinkle with lime zest, salt, pepper and 1/4 of parsley. Divide dates equally among chops, spreading a thin layer over one side of open chop. Sprinkle with chile. Fold over chops, enclosing stuffing. Sprinkle with sesame seeds and season again with salt, pepper, and a little more parsley.

Heat oil in large skillet over high. Sear pork chops until golden on both sides, about 1 minute each side. Transfer to small roasting pan or sheet and bake for 14 to 16 minutes, until juices run clear but chops are still moist. Remove immediately.

Meanwhile, in same skillet, combine remaining ginger and garlic and return to medium heat. (If no oil remains in pan, add 5 mL/1 tsp vegetable oil.) Sauté until golden and soft. Add lime juice, rum, molasses, and chicken stock. Simmer, uncovered, until reduced by 1/3 and slightly thickened, about 6 to 8 minutes.

Drizzle sauce over pork chops and sprinkle with remaining parsley and coriander, if desired. Serve with fried zucchini with toasted pistachios.

Pork Tenderloin with Apple Compote

Pork chops and applesauce are an age-old combination. I'm giving them a modern makeover by using pork tenderloin, wrapping it in smoky pancetta, then preparing my own spicy apple compote to accompany it. This is an ultra simple dish that the whole family will love.

2	pork tenderloins (about 3/4 lb/341 g each)	2
	Pepper, to taste	
	Several sprigs fresh thyme, chopped	
	Several leaves fresh sage, chopped	
8	thin slices pancetta or regular bacon	8
1 tbsp	vegetable oil	15 mL

Apple compote

2 tsp	vegetable oil	10 mL
1	large onion, diced	1
2	medium Granny Smith or Matsu apples, peeled, cored, and diced	2
	Juice and zest of 1 lemon	
1/2 cup	brown sugar	125 mL
1/4 cup	raisins	50 mL
1	clove	1
2 tbsp	apple cider vinegar	30 mL
	Salt and pepper, to taste	

Preheat oven to 180°C (350°F).

Rub pork generously with pepper, thyme, and sage. Wrap with pancetta and tie with butcher's twine. Sear in hot pan in oil until evenly browned on all sides. Place pork in roasting pan and finish cooking in oven for 15 minutes, or until done to preference.

To prepare compote, heat oil in medium skillet and add onion. Sauté over medium heat until soft, about 4 minutes. Add apples and continue to sauté, increasing heat to high. Cook apples for 5 minutes, or until soft. Add remaining ingredients and reduce heat to low. Simmer for 5 to 8 minutes. Remove from heat and serve with pork.

PREP

- The easiest way to tie the tenderloin is to cut four equal lengths of butcher's twine, each about 15 cm (6 in) long. Once the pork is seasoned and wrapped in pancetta, tie each piece of twine equal distances apart, securing the bacon.

- If you want apple compote that is very soft like applesauce, use McIntosh or Golden Delicious apples that are soft and will cook down.

OPTION

- You can also make pear compote by replacing the apples with ripe, firm pears.

Ginger-Crusted Pork Stir-Fry with Beet and Apple Batons

Serves 4

This dish is a full meal, including starch and leafy green. There are many ingredients, but the method is quite simple.

1	pork tenderloin	*1*
1	1-in/2.5-cm piece of ginger, grated	*1*
2	cloves garlic, chopped	*2*
	Several drops hot sauce	
1 tsp	hoisin sauce	*5 mL*
2	beets, with greens	*2*
2 tbsp	butter	*30 mL*
2	Granny Smith apples, cored and cut into batons	*2*
2	medium Yukon Gold potatoes, peeled and quartered	*2*
1	large onion, sliced	*1*
4	shiitake mushrooms, stems removed, diced	*4*
1/2	each red pepper and yellow pepper, diced	*1/2*
	Salt and pepper, to taste	
2 tbsp	vegetable oil	*30 mL*
1/4 cup	soy sauce	*50 mL*

PREP

- In this recipe, organization is the key to success. You'll find it easier to work on all the mini recipes at once so that your stir-fry comes together very quickly. Start with the beets so they're cooking while you put the potatoes on. That will give you ample time to chop the remaining ingredients.

- The pork should be cooked through, but should not resemble shoe leather.

OPTIONS

- The beet greens are optional, but they add lots of flavour.

- You can eliminate the beets altogether and substitute some Asian greens.

- Since this is a stir-fry, feel free to give it your own signature.

Slice pork thinly across the grain. Toss with 1/2 the ginger, 1/2 the garlic, hot sauce, and hoisin sauce. Meanwhile, trim beets, saving the greens. Cover with cold water and bring to a boil. Simmer for 8 to 10 minutes, or until just tender. Immerse in cold water and peel. Cut into batons. In small saucepan, heat 10 mL (2 tsp) butter and sauté beet and apple batons with remaining ginger until jammy, about 4 to 5 minutes. Set aside.

Boil potatoes in salted water for 8 to 10 minutes, or until just tender. Drain. In medium skillet, heat remaining butter and add onions and remaining garlic. Sauté until golden. Add mushrooms and peppers and sauté until soft, about 3 to 4 minutes. Mash potatoes very gently with fork, just to break them. Add to skillet with pepper mixture. Sauté until golden. Season with salt and pepper.

Heat oil in large wok or frying pan. Over high heat, stir-fry pork until just golden, working quickly. Add soy sauce and toss. Add beet greens and toss until just wilted. Serve pork with potato sauté and top with beet and apple mixture.

Vanilla Bourbon Baked Ham

I assure you this is the best ham recipe I have ever made. Although ham usually is only made for special occasions, it's so delicious I embarked on a mission to simplify the process. Can you imagine vanilla and bourbon brushed liberally over a ham? It's as incredible as it sounds—and it's easy.

1	vanilla bean, seeds scraped	*1*
1 tbsp	Dijon mustard	*15 mL*
1/2 cup	bourbon whisky	*125 mL*
3 tbsp	brown sugar	*45 mL*
	Cayenne pepper, to taste	
1	small boneless ham (about 3 lb/1.4 kg), cured and cooked (look for "heat and serve")	*1*
1 tbsp	butter	*15 mL*

Preheat oven to 180°C (350°F).

Combine all ingredients, except butter and ham, in small bowl and stir to blend.

Brush generously over ham and reserve remaining glaze. Place ham in small roasting pan. Pour in 50 mL (1/4 cup) of remaining marinade. Cover tightly with foil. Bake for 20 minutes, or until warmed through.

Remove foil and brush with remaining glaze. Increase heat to 200°C (400°F) and bake until glaze is browned, about 10 minutes.

Drain any remaining sauce from ham and transfer to small saucepan. Add butter and reduce for 5 minutes, or until just thick and glossy.

Serve with Potato and Celery Root Gratin (see page 44).

Serves 6 to 8

PREP

- The perfect mate for this recipe is Potato and Celery Root Gratin (see page 44). The timing is perfect for baking them at the same time.

- You want to use a baking ham, not a black forest ham for slicing. Since the ham is cured and completely cooked, all you're really doing is creating flavour and heating it in the oven.

OPTIONS

- If you have more time, you can try this with a fresh ham.

- The vanilla bean can be purchased at specialty gourmet shops, but you can substitute vanilla extract. Use about 10 mL (2 tsp) to replace the bean. And, please, never use artificial vanilla—you don't even want to know what it's made of.

Grilled Striploin
of Beef with Chimichurri

Serves 4

Chimichurri is a very simple condiment used in Argentina with just about any kind of beef preparation. I have altered it slightly, but it is still a very robust, spicy sauce that is served raw beside the meat instead of cooked into it. Chimichurri is a variation of an Italian salsa verde and shows the Italian influence on food in Buenos Aires.

	Vegetable oil (for wiping grill)	
4	beef striploin steaks (about 7 oz/199 g each), trimmed of excess fat	4
	Salt, to taste	
2 tsp	fresh rosemary, finely chopped *10 mL*	

Chimichurri

1/3 cup	coarsely chopped fresh parsley *75 mL*
2 tbsp	coarsely chopped fresh coriander *30 mL*
	Grated zest of 1 lemon
1 tsp	dried oregano *5 mL*
4	cloves garlic, chopped *4*
1/2	small Thai chile, minced *1/2*
1/3 cup	extra virgin olive oil *75 mL*
2 tbsp	red wine vinegar *30 mL*
	Juice of 1/2 lemon
	Salt, to taste

PREP

• Once the chimichurri is ready, this recipe is a simple steak with some fresh rosemary added.

• Leftover chimichurri can be covered and stored in the fridge for a few days and used in a beef stir-fry.

OPTION

• You can serve this sauce with grilled fish, but it should be fish with intensity, such as swordfish or calamari.

To make chimichurri, combine parsley, coriander, lemon zest, oregano, garlic, and chile in food processor and pulse until well combined. Add olive oil, vinegar, lemon juice, and salt and blend until smooth. Cover and set aside until ready to cook beef.

To cook meat, preheat grill on high and brush well. Wipe with vegetable oil. Season beef with salt and sprinkle with rosemary. Grill for 4 minutes per side, turning once, or until done to taste.

Serve steaks with chimichurri on the side and your favourite grilled vegetables.

Roasted Fillet of Beef with Burgundy Gastrique

Don't be alarmed by the name of this beef dish. It's my way of introducing you to the flavours of boeuf Bourgignon—a specialty in Burgundy that is slow-braised for hours. Short cuts are my department, however, and all you have to do is follow these simple instructions. A gastrique is a French base for a sauce that combines caramel and vinegar—a simple sweet and sour sauce. I made this dish for a couple of delightful guests in our studio when we were taping the show and they loved it.

1	beef tenderloin (about 2-1/2 lb/1.14 kg)	*1*
1 tbsp	Dijon mustard	*15 mL*
	Zest of 1 orange	
2	sprigs fresh rosemary, finely chopped	*2*
3	sprigs fresh thyme, finely chopped	*3*
2	cloves garlic, minced	*2*
1 tsp	freshly cracked black pepper	*5 mL*
	Salt, to taste	
1 tsp	vegetable oil	*5 mL*

Sauce

1 tbsp	butter	*15 mL*
6	shallots, finely sliced	*6*
2 tbsp	sugar	*30 mL*
2 tbsp	red wine vinegar	*30 mL*
1/2 cup	red Burgundy wine (other dry red wine can be substituted)	*125 mL*
1 cup	beef broth	*250 mL*
1	sprig thyme	*1*
1	bay leaf	*1*

Serves 6 to 8

PREP

- When cooking the shallots, low heat is best, as you want to slowly render the sugars without burning them.

- You can rub the tenderloin with seasonings and keep it covered in the fridge until ready to cook.

OPTION

- If you have lots of time on a weekend and you want to try a classical Burgundian beef, simply buy a shoulder or any braising cut of beef. Marinate in a bottle of red wine, preferably from Burgundy, then improvise with the remaining ingredients, keeping in mind that the meat needs to braise for several hours.

Preheat oven to 190°C (375°F).

Trim excess fat from beef. Combine remaining ingredients for beef, except salt and oil, in bowl and blend. Rub generously over meat. Season with salt. Heat large skillet on high and add oil. Add beef and sear all sides, turning often until browned, about 5 minutes. Transfer beef to small roasting pan and roast in oven for 20 to 25 minutes, or until done to your liking. *(continues)*

Meanwhile, using same skillet that beef was seared in, heat butter on low. Add shallots and sauté until very soft and brown, about 15 minutes. Stir frequently. Remove shallots from pan and reserve. Immediately add sugar and return to heat until sugar begins to turn amber. Remove from heat and add vinegar. Add back shallots and remaining ingredients and bring to a boil. Reduce heat to low and simmer, uncovered, until reduced by 1/3, about 15 to 20 minutes.

When beef is cooked, remove from oven and let rest 5 minutes. Slice and serve with sauce and Lemon Rosemary Green Beans (see page 60).

Spicy Stir-Fried Beef over Rice Noodles

Serves 6 to 8

PREP

- This is the perfect recipe for people who like meat but don't want to eat a big slab of it. The vegetables and rice noodles make up a huge part of the dish.

- Since the noodles are served at room temperature, you can soak them, season them, and set them aside until your stir-fry is prepared.

This stir-fry is a hot and spicy concoction of beef with many delicious and colourful vegetables. I'm always babbling to teenagers about eating their veggies because that makes for adults with great eating habits. If some members of your household are picky eaters, let them each pick one vegetable to remove. I'm full of bright ideas, in case you hadn't noticed. My motto is: What they don't know can't hurt them.

12 oz	sliced beef striploin or tenderloin	*340 g*
2 tsp	tamarind paste	*10 mL*
	Zest of 1 orange	
1 tsp	ground fennel seed	*5 mL*
Pinch	allspice	*Pinch*
1	small cayenne or Thai chile, chopped	*1*
2 tbsp	vegetable oil	*30 mL*
	Several drops sesame oil	
1	onion, sliced	*1*
2	cloves garlic, sliced	*2*
6	snow peas, sliced diagonally	*6*
1	red pepper, sliced	*1*
1/4 cup	soy sauce	*50 mL*
1/4 cup	roasted peanuts	*50 mL*
1/4 cup	bean sprouts	*50 mL*

Rice noodles

8 oz	vermicelli rice noodles	*227 g*
1/4 cup	orange juice	*50 mL*
2 tbsp	rice wine vinegar	*30 mL*
2 tbsp	soy sauce	*30 mL*
	Several drops sesame oil	
2	green onions, chopped	*2*
2	carrots, grated	*2*

In bowl, combine beef with tamarind and spices. Toss well to coat.

Soak rice noodles in hot, but not boiling, water for 30 minutes. Remove and drain well. Combine orange juice, vinegar, soy sauce, and sesame oil and toss with noodles. Cover and set aside until beef is cooked.

In wok or large skillet, heat vegetable and sesame oils. Add onion and garlic and toss for 2 to 3 minutes, or until soft. Add beef and continue to stir-fry on very high heat until beef is lightly browned. Add snow peas, red pepper, and soy sauce and toss gently for 1 minute. Remove from heat and sprinkle with peanuts and sprouts.

Combine noodles with carrots and green onions and spoon warm beef mixture over top.

OPTIONS

• The world is your oyster—in this recipe you can use any vegetables you like.

• This recipe works beautifully with beef. If you want to try it with chicken, eliminate the orange zest and the tamarind and add a little lime juice instead.

Vietnamese Beef Broth—Pho

Serves 4 to 6

I refer to this recipe as my pseudo pho because this isn't exactly how it's made in Vietnam. The secret to this soup is in the broth. If you have time to make a homemade stock, see the Mise en Place section for recipes. The best part of this soup is the ritual of eating it. I end up wearing half the noodles, not to mention the broth. It's very light and tastes fresh because of the basil and bean sprouts added just before serving.

8 cups	beef stock	*2 L*
1	5-cm (2-in) piece of ginger, peeled and grated	*1*
1	large stick cinnamon	*1*
3/4 tsp	coriander seeds, gently crushed	*3 mL*
2	pieces star anise	*2*
1 tsp	each sugar and freshly cracked black pepper	*5 mL*
2 tsp	Asian fish sauce like nuoc mam or nam pla	10 mL
1	pkg (1 lb/454 g) rice noodles, flat and thick	*1*
1/4 cup	chopped fresh coriander	*50 mL*
4	large shallots, finely sliced (or 1 onion)	*4*
10 oz	beef tenderloin, thinly sliced	*284 g*

Garnish

Bean sprouts and fresh basil leaves

2 limes, quartered

Fresh Thai chiles, finely sliced

Hoisin and chile sauce

PREP

- Normally, this dish is made with tripe and beef tendon. I am refining it somewhat by using tenderloin, but I prefer it this way. To help you slice the tenderloin very thinly, place it in the freezer for about 15 minutes before serving and use a very sharp non-serrated knife.
- The fish sauce can be found in Asian specialty markets.
- Do not cook the noodles too long or they will be mushy.

OPTION

- Use striploin or sirloin if you don't want to spend too much on tenderloin.

In large pot, combine stock, ginger, cinnamon, coriander, and star anise. Bring to a boil and reduce heat to low. Simmer, uncovered, for 20 minutes. Add sugar, pepper, and fish sauce. Adjust seasoning. Strain and keep warm over low heat.

Cook rice noodles until al dente, about 3 minutes, in salted boiling water. Drain. Divide noodles among bowls. Cover with coriander, shallots, and beef. Pour hot broth over noodles. Garnish with remaining ingredients. Meat will cook to rare in the boiling broth.

Roasted Veal Loin with Wild Mushroom and Port Glaze

This veal loin is simple enough to make for an everyday dinner, yet impressive enough to serve to any guest. The combination of sweet port and earthy wild mushrooms gives the veal a perfectly balanced sauce.

1 tbsp	vegetable oil	*15 mL*
1	veal loin or striploin (about 1-1/2 lb/681 g)	*1*
	Salt and freshly cracked black pepper, to taste	
2 tbsp	chopped fresh tarragon	*30 mL*
2	cloves garlic, minced	*2*

Glaze

4 cups	chicken or veal stock	*1 L*
1 cup	Port or Madeira	*250 mL*
4	small shallots, sliced	*4*
2	cloves garlic, crushed	*2*
1/8 oz	dried mushrooms, soaked	*3.5 g*
1	sprig fresh tarragon	*1*

To prepare sauce, combine all ingredients in medium saucepan and bring to a boil over high heat. Lower heat to medium and reduce sauce to 1/4 its original volume, about 35 minutes.

Preheat oven to 190°C (375°F).

Over high heat, in large skillet, heat vegetable oil. Rub veal with salt, pepper, tarragon, and garlic. Sear veal on all sides to brown, about 5 minutes. Transfer veal to roasting pan and roast in oven for 30 to 35 minutes, or until done to your liking. Let it rest for 5 minutes before slicing.

Strain sauce and serve over slices of veal.

Serves 4

PREP

- Practise checking if meat is cooked by pressing down on it with tongs. It should feel springy but not completely tough. The veal is quite lean, so cooking it beyond medium will give you a dry piece of meat.

- Use your timer as a guide and check the meat to ensure that it is still juicy. Always let it rest before slicing.

- Frozen stock comes in handy for creating a simple sauce that is loaded with flavour.

- Dried mushrooms are expensive, but you need a very small amount to develop flavour. Always wash them thoroughly before using, because they hold a lot of sand.

OPTION

- You can make this recipe with veal chops instead of a loin and serve it with some mashed potatoes or polenta.

Roasted Veal Tenderloin on Garlic-Rubbed Crostini

Serves 4 to 6 as an appetizer

This is a very personal recipe, because I developed it for a dinner with a group of friends. We get together on a regular basis and each couple has to make a course. I was in charge of the appetizer and I didn't want to fence myself in, so I went to the market not knowing what I was going to make. I walked around and selected ingredients and this is what I came up with. The group went crazy over this creation, so I thought I'd share it with you. Strictly speaking, it's an appetizer, but I think it belongs in the meat section.

1	veal tenderloin (about 1 lb/454 g)	1
1 tbsp	fresh thyme, chopped	15 mL
1 tbsp	fresh tarragon, chopped	15 mL
1 tsp	Dijon mustard	5 mL
	Salt and pepper, to taste	
1/4 cup + 2 tbsp	olive oil	80 mL
2	small eggplants, finely diced	2
2	cloves garlic, 1 clove minced, 1 clove whole	2
1 tsp	balsamic vinegar	5 mL
1	baguette, sliced and toasted	1
3 oz	pecorino crotonese cheese, sliced (for garnish)	85 g

Preheat oven to 180°C (350°F).

Rub veal with herbs and mustard and season with salt and pepper. Sear in small pan over medium-high heat in 5 mL (1 tsp) olive oil until golden on all sides. Finish cooking veal in oven for 10 minutes, or until medium. Remove and let rest for 5 minutes.

Meanwhile, heat 25 mL (5 tsp) olive oil in medium skillet. Add eggplant and sauté until lightly browned. Add minced garlic and toss for a few minutes, or until soft. Add balsamic vinegar and pepper. Remove from heat and cool.

Drizzle bread slices with 50 mL (1/4 cup) olive oil and rub with whole clove garlic. Slice veal and lay 1 to 2 slices on top of toast. Top with 5 mL (1 tsp) of sautéed eggplant and finish with a slice of cheese.

PREP

- Pecorino is a sheep's milk cheese available at specialty cheese shops.
- If you don't have a cheese slicer, use a vegetable peeler.
- This appetizer is great served warm or at room temperature.
- You can make the toast, rub it with garlic, and set it aside.
- While the veal is roasting, you have just enough time to make the eggplant mixture.

OPTIONS

- If you can't find pecorino, use good-quality Parmesan cheese instead.
- Beef can be used instead of veal; simply adjust your cooking time depending on the size of the tenderloin.

Quick Polenta with Veal Chop and Portobello Mushrooms

In North America we have access to just about any ingredient on the planet. We can also enjoy cooking dishes that would have taken our ancestors hours to prepare. One of my latest finds is a quick-cooking polenta that's ready in 5 minutes. I like to cook the polenta so it's soft and creamy, and to make it even creamier I have added some Gorgonzola. The polenta is the canvas for the simple veal chop, which is oven-baked on a bed of Portobello mushrooms.

4	veal chops	4
2	cloves garlic, minced	2
	Zest of 1 lemon, grated	
1 tbsp	chopped fresh rosemary	15 mL
	Salt and freshly cracked black pepper, to taste	
2 tbsp	olive oil	30 mL
2	large Portobello mushrooms, diced	2
2-3/4 cups	chicken stock or water	675 mL
1/2 cup	quick-cooking polenta	125 mL
2 oz	Gorgonzola cheese, crumbled	57 g

Rub veal chops with garlic, lemon zest, and rosemary. Season with salt and pepper.

Preheat oven to 200°C (400°F). Place empty roasting pan in oven and heat for 5 minutes. Pour in 15 mL (1 tbsp) olive oil. Lay chops in pan in single layer. Sprinkle mushrooms over top. Bake for 12 to 15 minutes, turning once.

Meanwhile, bring stock and remaining olive oil to a rapid boil in large heavy-bottom pot. Season with salt and pepper. Pour in polenta in slow, steady stream, mixing vigorously with wooden spoon. Keep stirring until mixture is bubbling.

To serve, divide polenta among 4 plates and sprinkle with Gorgonzola. Lay veal chop on top and spoon mushrooms and pan juices over top.

Serves 4

PREP

- Regular polenta will take at least 20 minutes of stirring to cook it properly.

- For proper timing, prepare the veal chops, set them aside, then boil the stock for the polenta. While the chops are in the oven, you can cook the polenta and both dishes will be ready at the same time.

- If polenta sits for a few minutes it will get stiffer, so let it cook for the minimum time to keep in the moisture.

OPTION

- For a different twist on the polenta, reduce the stock to 625 mL (2-1/2 cups) and cook it longer until more firm. Spread it on a medium baking pan in 2.5-cm (1-in) layer and let cool. Chill and slice the polenta, crumble the Gorgonzola over top, and broil it to melt the cheese before serving.

Veal Cutlets with Sweet Potato and Yukon Gold Pancakes

Serves 4

Cutlets are a very simple way to have dinner ready in minutes. The potato pancakes cook in 3 to 5 minutes, so time is not going to be a problem with this recipe. The cutlets are also great because you can store them in the fridge seasoned and ready to fry if you know someone will be home late.

1/4 cup	flour	*50 mL*
1/4 cup	breadcrumbs	*50 mL*
1/3 cup	chopped and blended fresh parsley and tarragon	*75 mL*
4	veal cutlets (Provimi), each about 6 oz/170 g, cut from fillet portion of leg	*4*
1/4 cup	milk	*50 mL*
1	egg, beaten	*1*
2	large Yukon Gold potatoes, peeled and grated	*2*
1	small sweet potato, peeled and grated	*1*
1/4 cup	chopped fresh chives	*50 mL*
	Salt and freshly cracked black pepper, to taste	
	Vegetable oil (for frying)	

PREP

- Putting the herbs in the breadcrumb mixture ensures even distribution over cutlets.

OPTIONS

- If you don't want to make the potato pancakes, see the many other potato recipes in this book.
- You could also make turkey or chicken cutlets, following this same recipe, but you need to ensure that they are cooked all the way through. Veal can be served medium rare.

Spread flour on baking sheet. Mix breadcrumbs and herbs and spread on another baking sheet. Dip cutlets in milk and then in flour, and lightly tap off excess. Dip in egg and then in breadcrumb mixture. Stack cutlets, separated by parchment paper or plastic wrap, cover with plastic, and refrigerate until ready to cook.

Meanwhile, combine potato, sweet potato, and chives. Season with salt and pepper. Heat about 50 mL (1/4 cup) oil in large skillet and divide potato mixture into 4 mounds. Press each mound into 12.5-cm (5-in) circle. Cook for 3 minutes, or until potatoes hold together and are golden. Flip and cook other side. Remove from pan and add more oil.

Fry cutlets for 2 to 3 minutes per side, or until golden. Remove from heat.

Serve with your favourite vegetables.

Harissa Seared Lamb Chops

Serves 4

The story that surrounds this recipe remains one of my favourite from the show. Our prop master, Todd, came into the studio and asked who Harissa was (the recipe says, "For Harissa"). I laughed and told him that Harissa is a sauce, not a person. Harissa is a Tunisian chile sauce that is served a multitude of ways. I have chosen to rub it on the lamb before cooking.

8	medium lamb chops (rib or loin)	8
	Salt, to taste	

For Harissa

2	medium dried New Mexico chiles, soaked for 15 minutes in warm water	2
3	cloves garlic, minced	3
1 tsp	honey	5 mL
1/2 tsp	coriander seed, ground	2 mL
3/4 tsp	cumin seed, ground	3 mL
1/4 tsp	caraway seed, ground	1 mL
1/4 cup	extra virgin olive oil	50 mL
1/4 cup	chopped fresh mint	50 mL

PREP
- Chiles need to be thoroughly soaked and then drained before they can be puréed with remaining ingredients.
- The Harissa keeps very well for several days if covered in the fridge.

OPTION
- This Harissa can be served with chicken instead of lamb. To serve with beef, change the mint to parsley.

Preheat grill to high.

To make Harissa, drain chiles well and chop. Combine with garlic, honey, spices, and olive oil in food processor. Pulse until smooth. Add mint and pulse to combine.

Rub salted lamb chops with paste, brushing lightly. Do not use too much paste or chops will be too spicy. Extra paste can be served on the side to increase heat. Cover and save any leftover paste in fridge for later use.

Grill chops for 4 to 5 minutes per side, depending on thickness, until medium.

Accompany with favourite vegetables and couscous.

Moroccan Crusted
Lamb Racks with Grilled Apricots

Serves 4

Lamb racks are the most tender and best-looking cut of the meat, but they are quite expensive. I would save these for a special occasion and just use regular chops for everyday use. The most unusual part of this recipe is the combination of pomegranate molasses and chopped mint, which is drizzled over the lamb after slicing. And then there are the fresh grilled apricots, which add a sweet and tangy contrast to the game and spice of the lamb. Once again, you're getting a very elaborate description for a simple dish.

2	lamb racks, trimmed	2
	Salt, to taste	
1-2 tbsp	olive oil	15-30 mL
8	ripe whole apricots, cut in half, stones removed	8
2 tbsp	pomegranate molasses	30 mL
1/2 cup	fresh mint, chopped	125 mL

Rub

2 tbsp	olive oil	30 mL
2	large cloves garlic, minced	2
1/4 cup	chopped fresh parsley	50 mL
1 tbsp	whole cumin seed, crushed	15 mL
2 tsp	whole coriander seed, crushed	10 mL
1	small chile, finely chopped	1
1/2 tsp	ground cinnamon	2 mL
Pinch	ground cardamom	Pinch
1 tsp	freshly cracked black pepper	5 mL

PREP
- When buying lamb racks, make sure they are "Frenched." Ask the butcher to remove the chine bone. That will allow you to cut through the chops very easily.
- Pomegranate molasses is a tangy syrup that is available at any Middle Eastern specialty shop.
- The yoghurt sauce keeps very well for several days if covered in the fridge.

In food processor, combine all ingredients for rub and pulse until blended. Rub over both racks generously. Season with salt.

Preheat oven to 190°C (375°F).

In large skillet, heat olive oil on high. Sear racks on all sides until well browned, about 4 to 5 minutes. Transfer lamb to roasting pan and continue to cook in oven for 17 to 20 minutes, or until medium (internal temperature of 60°C/140°F).

Grill apricots for 3 minutes per side, or until golden but still firm.

Combine molasses and mint in medium bowl. When racks are cooked, remove from oven and let rest for 5 minutes, covered with foil, before slicing. Slice and dip exposed sides in mint mixture.

Serve with grilled apricots and drizzled with yoghurt sauce, if desired.

Yoghurt Sauce

1/2 cup	plain yoghurt	*125 mL*
1 tsp	honey	*5 mL*
2 tbsp	chopped fresh mint	*30 mL*
1/2 tsp	ground toasted cumin seeds	*2 mL*
	Zest of 1 lime, grated	
Pinch	ground cinnamon	*Pinch*

Combine all ingredients in medium bowl. Stir, cover, and chill until ready to serve.

OPTIONS

- You can sear the apricots in a pan if you don't have access to a grill. You simply want to caramelize some of the sugar for a golden crust.

- The yoghurt sauce is also delicious when drizzled over fresh fruit.

Curry Seared Lamb Chops with Toasted Cumin Basmati Rice

Serves 4

In my continual efforts to simplify your cooking experiences, I have created this recipe because I love the flavour of curry. But most often it requires a slow cooking process. Here, you will be able to enjoy your very own curry blend that will come together in minutes. You can always buy a prepared curry blend, but that locks you into a specific combination. On a weekend, or if you are just in the mood, you can always create another curry recipe in this book that is stewed.

PREP

- For maximum flavour, toast the spices whole in a dry skillet by tossing for 2 minutes until lightly browned. Then grind in mortar and pestle and add to ginger and other ingredients.

OPTIONS

- You can add currants or blond raisins to the rice for texture and a sweeter flavour.

- This curry is a great spice blend for a rack of lamb for a more formal occasion.

2	cloves garlic, minced	2
1/4 tsp	turmeric	1 mL
1/2 tsp	coriander seed, ground	2 mL
1/2 tsp	cumin seed, ground	2 mL
2	Thai chiles, finely chopped	2
1/2 tsp	mustard seed, ground	2 mL
1/4 tsp	cloves	1 mL
1/4 tsp	cinnamon	1 mL
1/4 tsp	ground ginger	1 mL
8	medium lamb chops	8
	Salt and pepper, to taste	
1 tbsp	olive oil	15 mL

Rice

1 cup	basmati rice, rinsed	250 mL
1-3/4 cup	chicken stock	425 mL
1 tbsp	olive oil	15 mL
1	cinnamon stick	1
1 tsp	whole cumin seed, toasted and ground	5 mL
1	small red pepper, diced	1
	Salt and pepper, to taste	

Preheat oven to 190°C (375°F).

Combine all ingredients for rice in heavy-bottom saucepan. Bring to a boil and reduce heat to low. Cover and simmer for 14 minutes. Do not remove lid. Remove from heat and let stand for 5 minutes. Fluff with fork and serve with lamb chops.

Meanwhile, combine ingredients for curry and rub over lamb. Season with salt and pepper.

Heat oil in ovenproof pan until hot. Sear chops 2 minutes on each side, or until golden. Remove and finish cooking in oven for 10 to 12 minutes, or until done to your liking, depending on thickness of lamb.

Lamb Kofta
with Romesco Sauce

To continue my culinary world tour, this recipe combines the oval-shaped lamb kofta of the Middle East with a traditional Spanish red pepper and hazelnut paste. Food should never be boring. In this case, by using ground lamb instead of beef and by shaping it into a mini football instead of a round ball, you have kofta. When served with a saffron or turmeric pilaf, it makes for a very dramatic presentation with very pronounced colour.

1 lb	lean ground lamb	*454 g*
6	green onions, chopped	*6*
1/2 cup	coarsely chopped fresh parsley	*125 mL*
1/2 tsp	allspice	*2 mL*
1/4 cup	coarsely chopped fresh mint	*50 mL*
1	clove garlic, minced	*1*
	Salt, to taste	
2 tbsp	olive oil	*30 mL*

Serves 4

PREP

- If using lamb that you ground yourself or had specially ground, kofta can be cooked medium; otherwise, they should be well done.

- Kofta can be shaped and stored, covered, in the fridge until you want to prepare dinner.

- Once you have added the bread and nuts to the sauce, you simply need to pulse the processor, otherwise the sauce may start to separate.

Sauce

1	red pepper, roasted and peeled	*1*
1/2 cup	roma tomatoes, chopped (canned, without juice)	*125 mL*
1	slice rustic bread	*1*
1/4 cup	whole hazelnuts, skin off	*50 mL*
2	cloves garlic, chopped	*2*
Pinch	cayenne	*Pinch*
1-1/2 tbsp	olive oil	*22 mL*
1/3 cup	extra virgin olive oil	*75 mL*
	Salt and pepper, to taste	
	Lemon juice (optional)	

To prepare the sauce, purée red pepper in food processor. Cook tomatoes in small saucepan on low heat, until very dry, stirring frequently, about 6 to 8 minutes. Cool.

Meanwhile, fry bread in small skillet until golden on both sides. Remove from pan and cool slightly. In same pan, toast hazelnuts until golden.

Add bread and hazelnuts to puréed red pepper and pulse until smooth. Add cooled tomatoes, garlic, and cayenne and pulse. With machine running, pour olive oil in a steady stream until smooth. Do not overwork or sauce will split. Season with salt and pepper and a touch of lemon juice, if desired. Cover and set aside until kofta are cooked.

Preheat oven to 190°C (375°F).

To prepare kofta, combine all ingredients, except oil, in medium bowl. Work gently with hands just until mixture holds together. Shape meat into 10 to 12 medium football-shaped ovals.

Heat olive oil in large skillet on high. Fry kofta for 4 minutes, or until browned on all sides, turning as needed. Transfer to baking sheet or roasting pan and bake for 10 to 12 minutes, or until juices run clear.

Serve with sauce and your favourite rice.

Dishing Out the Pizza and Pasta

Roasted Tomato and Basil Pesto

Makes 1-1/2 cups

This is yet another variation on a classical pesto. I have slow-roasted simple plum tomatoes in a moderate oven. This intensifies their flavour and adds a whole new dimension to an ordinary pesto. Restaurants sometimes dry the tomatoes overnight in an oven at very low heat (80°C/175°F) to slowly lose the moisture but capture the wonderful flavours of oven-dried tomatoes. This is a great make-ahead project that can be a great addition to things you pull out of the freezer when in need. Remember: A little work today can save you a lot of time tomorrow. I don't know who said that, but it makes sense.

1-1/2 lb	medium plum tomatoes (about 8-10)	*681 g*
1 tbsp	olive oil	*15 mL*
1 tsp	dried oregano	*5 mL*
	Salt and freshly cracked black pepper, to taste	
2	cloves garlic	*2*
1 cup	fresh basil (1 large bunch)	*250 mL*
1/2 cup	Parmesan cheese	*125 mL*
1/2 cup	olive oil	*125 mL*

Preheat oven to 135°C (275°F). Cut tomatoes in half, lengthwise, and place on roasting pan, skin side down, so that liquid can fall into tray below. Brush lightly with 15 mL (1 tbsp) olive oil, sprinkle with oregano, and season with salt and pepper. Roast for 1 hour, or until tomatoes have reduced in size by about 1/3. Cool.

Combine remaining ingredients, except oil, with roasted tomatoes in a food processor and blend until smooth. With machine on, add oil in steady stream. Pesto will keep in the refrigerator, covered, for a few days or in the freezer for a few weeks.

PREP

- Late summer is the ideal time for this project because beautiful basil and plum tomatoes are in season.
- You can make many batches or different kinds of pesto and freeze them in ice trays for easy retrieval in the cooler months. They're almost like pesto pops!

OPTION

- Serve this pesto with your favourite pasta or spoon it into a vegetable soup for instant flavour.

Grilled Beef and Vegetable Pasta

The beauty of this recipe is that you can use any vegetables that are in season. Grilling the beef and the vegetables adds complexity to the pasta and makes it quite different from anything you've tasted. Versatility is another great feature because you can make the whole dish and serve it warm or at room temperature for a picnic or summer luncheon. On the show, I developed the recipe the way it reads below, then just before taping came up with a variation to further improve it (see Option). Also note that you have pasta, vegetables, and meat all in one recipe.

1 lb	beef tenderloin	*454 g*
1 tbsp	each fresh thyme and basil, chopped	*15 mL*
1	large clove garlic, chopped	*1*
1 tbsp	Dijon mustard	*15 mL*
1	red pepper	*1*
1	small bunch asparagus, blanched	*1*
1	large onion, peeled	*1*
2	plum tomatoes, peeled	*2*
1/4 cup	olive oil	*50 mL*
1/4 cup	fresh basil, chopped	*50 mL*
8 oz	penne	*227 g*
	Salt and pepper, to taste	
1/4 cup	shaved Parmesan cheese, preferably Reggiano	*50 mL*

Serves 4

Preheat oven to 180°C (350°F).

Rub beef tenderloin with herbs, garlic, and mustard. Grill on high on barbecue for 4 minutes on each side. Place in roasting pan and continue to cook in oven for 20 minutes, or to preference. Let meat cool for 15 minutes and slice thinly. Meanwhile, grill vegetables for 3 minutes on each side, or until evenly browned. Remove and slice. Mix with 1/2 olive oil and some of the chopped basil.

Meanwhile, cook pasta in rolling, boiling water according to package directions. Drain and add remaining olive oil. Reserve.

Mix all ingredients together with pasta and adjust seasoning. Sprinkle with Parmesan cheese and more basil, if desired.

PREP

- Any stemmed or tough vegetable should be blanched before grilling. This allows the vegetable to become tender before burning. Peppers and tomatoes contain mostly water so they grill beautifully.

- I'm calling for 454 g (1 lb) of tenderloin. If you buy fillets already cut into steaks, there is no need to finish cooking them in the oven. Usually the tenderloin I purchase is cylindrical and takes a little time to cook through.

OPTION

- A great variation is to purée the red pepper and tomatoes, after grilling, into a chunky salsa. Add the remaining ingredients as per recipe for a room-temperature sauce.

Couscous

Here are two variations for couscous that you can use, depending on your needs. Contrary to popular opinion, couscous is a pasta, not a grain. It really should be cooked twice for a fluffy and plump texture, but I like to cheat and use the quick-cooking type. Couscous is an ideal side dish for any stew, curry, or even as an alternative to rice.

couscous with toasted almonds and apricots

2 tbsp	olive oil	*30 mL*
1/4 cup	chopped apricots	*50 mL*
	Salt and pepper, to taste	
1-3/4 cup	chicken stock or water	*425 mL*
1 cup	medium couscous (quick-cooking)	*250 mL*
1/4 cup	natural almonds, toasted and chopped	*50 mL*
2 tbsp	chopped fresh mint	*30 mL*

In medium saucepan, heat oil on medium. Add apricots, salt, and pepper. Stir and add stock. Bring to a boil on high. Add couscous and stir. Cover and remove from heat. Let stand for 5 minutes.

Remove lid and add almonds and mint. Fluff with fork to prevent sticking.

This recipe goes beautifully with Moroccan Vegetable Tagine (see page 62).

Serves 4

PREP

- Remove couscous from heat immediately after stirring or it will be mushy.

- Mint and almonds should not be added at the beginning or the almonds will be soggy and the mint will lose its fresh taste.

vegetable couscous

2 tbsp	olive oil	*30 mL*
1	onion, chopped	*1*
1	green onion, chopped	*1*
1	red pepper, diced	*1*
1	ear corn, husked and kernels removed	*1*
1	clove garlic, chopped	*1*
Pinch	saffron threads (optional)	*Pinch*
1/4 tsp	cumin seed	*1 mL*
Pinch	coriander seed	*Pinch*
Pinch	dried chile	*Pinch*
1-3/4 cups	chicken stock or water	*425 mL*
	Salt and freshly cracked black pepper, to taste	
1 cup	couscous (quick-cooking)	*250 mL*

Heat oil in medium saucepan over high heat. Add onion and sauté for 2 minutes, until soft. Add remaining vegetables and spices and sauté for 2 minutes, or until soft.

Add stock and season with salt and pepper. Bring to a boil. Add couscous and remove from heat. Stir and cover. Let stand 5 minutes.

Fluff with a fork and serve immediately.

Serves 4

PREP

- If you're making this dish for vegetarians, be sure to use vegetable stock or water.

- To remove corn kernels from cob, stand the husk on a board. Guide a knife from the top, working all the way down the cob. Corn kernels will fly around, but you will get most of them. Keep turning the cob and repeat process until all kernels are off.

OPTIONS

- Add some diced chicken meat to this dish for added flavour.

- Use frozen corn if you don't want to remove the kernels from the cob yourself.

Pasta with Grilled Chicken, Garlic, and Olives

Serves 4

This recipe is heavy on flavour but light on fat. It's also colourful, and only needs a simple salad on the side. For those of you looking for more protein, you can use four chicken breasts—one for each serving. Use penne or bow-tie pasta instead of spaghetti.

PREP

- When chicken is grilled, it's left slightly undercooked so it can be added later to the sauce and warmed through. Make sure that you cook the chicken completely through after adding it to the sauce.
- Do not use the same board to slice chicken and chop herbs or any other vegetable.

OPTIONS

- You can make the sauce starting with chicken breast thinly sliced, as though you were making a stir-fry. You must take the chicken out, add the tomatoes, etc., then add the chicken back when sauce is almost ready.
- Those who are wheat intolerant should use soy bean pasta, available at any health store.

1 tbsp +2 tsp	olive oil	*25 mL*
2	cloves garlic, chopped	*2*
2 tbsp	chopped fresh basil	*30 mL*
1 tbsp	chopped fresh thyme	*15 mL*
2	chicken breasts, boneless, skinless	*2*
	Salt and pepper, to taste	
1	small onion, chopped	*1*
4	plum tomatoes, diced	*4*
1	yellow pepper, chopped	*1*
1/4 cup	black olives, pitted	*50 mL*
1/2 cup	chicken stock	*125 mL*
1	small chile pepper, chopped	*1*
12 oz	dry pasta	*340 g*
	Parmesan cheese (optional)	

Combine 5 mL (1 tsp) olive oil and 1/2 each of garlic, basil, and thyme. Rub on whole chicken breasts and season with salt and pepper. Grill on barbecue for 3 minutes per side, until golden and firm. Remove and set aside.

In medium saucepan, heat 15 mL (1 tbsp) olive oil, remaining garlic, and onion and sauté for 3 minutes, or until soft. Add tomatoes, yellow pepper, olives, stock, remaining thyme, and chile pepper. Cook for 5 minutes on medium heat, until sauce is slightly thickened.

Meanwhile, cook pasta in lots of boiling, salted water according to package directions for al dente pasta. Drain and toss in remaining olive oil.

Slice chicken breast and add to sauce. Season with salt and pepper, add remaining basil, and simmer for 3 minutes, until chicken is cooked through. Add pasta and toss until warmed through. Sprinkle with Parmesan cheese, if desired.

Linguine with Toasted Almond Cream Pesto

You'll be pleasantly surprised by this unique almond pesto. I toast whole skin-on almonds, then coarsely chop them. I sprinkle them on the pasta at the end instead of blending them into the pesto. This gives a great crunchy texture with a nutty taste. Also, the tomatoes are chopped and sprinkled on raw at the end. They give the dish a cool, refreshing contrast to the creamy pesto. Put a bookmark on this recipe.

2	cloves garlic, minced	2
1	small bunch basil, stems removed, washed well	1
1/4 cup	extra virgin olive oil	50 mL
	Salt and freshly cracked black pepper, to taste	
2 tbsp	35% cream (optional)	30 mL
1 lb	linguine	454 g
1	large field tomato, diced	1
1/4 cup	whole almonds, skin on, toasted and coarsely chopped	50 mL
	Freshly grated Parmesan cheese (Reggianno, preferably)	

Bring large pot of water to boil on high. Season liberally with salt.

Meanwhile, in a food processor combine garlic, basil, and olive oil and pulse until smooth. Season with salt and pepper. Add cream, if desired.

Cook pasta in boiling water for 8 to 10 minutes, or until al dente. Drain.

Toss immediately with pesto and sprinkle with tomato and almonds. Garnish with Parmesan cheese.

Serves 4 to 6

PREP

- For best results with pesto, make sure you wash the basil leaves thoroughly and spin dry or pat dry with tea towel.

- Adding the chopped nuts at the end gives a different texture to most pestos, because the nuts are not puréed.

- I usually call for 454 g (1 lb) of pasta in my recipes because most packages come that way. A portion should be about 85 g (3 oz) per person, so you can adjust accordingly.

OPTIONS

- Adding the cream will give the pesto a sweeter flavour and a creamy look. It also will add some animal fat, so the choice is yours.

- The cheese can be omitted if you're watching your animal fat intake.

- Of course, any kind of pasta can be used in place of the linguine.

Orecchiette with Arugula, Porcini, and Carmelized Shallots

Serves 4 to 6

PREP

- The flavour from this great pasta dish starts from slowly drawing out the natural sugars in the shallots. Once they are browned and soft, only then can you add the garlic so it doesn't burn. The flavours are further intensified by the dried mushrooms and the reduction of the stock and wine.

- The sauce can be made in advance and stored in the fridge for a couple of days. The pasta should always be cooked just before serving.

OPTIONS

- All dried wild mushrooms are found in upscale grocery stores in small plastic bags. You can use a fresh mushroom like shiitake, chanterelle, or Portobello instead.

- Use spinach in place of arugula.

I have to hand it to the Italians—they have thought of every possible shape and size for pasta. These little babies are called orecchiette (little ears), because they look like little ears. They are one of my favourite because the ends are a little thicker and stay crunchy. They also have little ridges that hold sauce very well. If you have run out of pasta recipes, this one offers an unusual stock and red wine-based sauce with wild mushroom and raw, chopped, peppery arugula at the end. I know you probably haven't made this one before. I call it Mike Tyson's favourite pasta.

3 tbsp	olive oil	*45 mL*
4	large shallots, sliced	*4*
2	sprigs fresh thyme	*2*
1	large clove garlic, chopped	*1*
2 oz	dried porcini mushrooms, soaked for 30 minutes in warm water	*57 g*
1/2 cup	red wine	*125 mL*
2 cups	good-quality chicken or veal stock	*500 mL*
1 lb	orecchiette pasta	*454 g*
1	bunch arugula, washed, trimmed, and chopped	*1*
	Salt and freshly cracked black pepper, to taste	
	Freshly grated Parmigiano Reggianno	

Heat olive oil over medium and sauté shallots and thyme for 10 minutes, stirring frequently. Shallots should be browned and soft. Add garlic and mushrooms and sauté for 3 minutes. Add wine and stock and bring to a boil. Reduce heat to low and simmer, uncovered, until reduced by half, about 15 minutes.

Meanwhile, cook pasta in large pot of boiling, salted water for 10 minutes, or until al dente. Drain and toss into sauce without rinsing. Sprinkle with arugula and season to taste. Serve immediately with freshly grated Parmigiano Reggianno.

Orzo with Zucchini, Eggplant, and Feta

Orzo is a pasta that is shaped like a long grain of rice. The Greek love orzo. It's cooked in the oven or on the stovetop, with chicken or lamb. When I burst into the house late some evenings, orzo is a simple thing I like to make. It's very versatile and you can add just about any vegetable to it. I also cook it like a pilaf and don't drain it. Just read through this recipe and all will be explained.

Serves 4

1/4 cup	olive oil	*50 mL*
2	baby eggplants, diced	*2*
3	shallots, chopped	*3*
2	large cloves garlic, chopped	*2*
2	large sprigs fresh thyme	*2*
1 tsp	dried Greek oregano	*5 mL*
4 cups	chicken stock	*1 L*
2 cups	orzo pasta	*500 mL*
1	large zucchini, diced	*1*
	Salt and pepper, to taste	
3 oz	crumbled feta cheese	*85 g*

In medium pot, heat 1/2 olive oil on high. Sauté eggplant, tossing vigorously until golden, about 5 minutes. Add remaining oil, shallots, and garlic and sauté on medium heat for 3 minutes, or until shallot is soft. Add thyme, oregano, and stock and stir.

Cover and simmer on medium heat for 6 minutes, or until stock is reduced by 1/3. Add orzo and zucchini, stir, and reduce heat to simmer, covered. Cook for 12 minutes, stirring occasionally. If after 8 minutes of cooking the liquid has been absorbed but orzo is not yet cooked, add 125 mL (1/2 cup) water, stir, and continue to cook. Remove from heat and check seasoning.

Sprinkle with feta cheese before serving.

PREP

- The trick with this recipe is to get a creamy texture with lots of flavour. Once you have added the stock, cover and reduce to a low simmer. Stir occasionally and test the orzo. If the orzo is still raw and moisture has evaporated, add a little boiling water to keep the temperature up and the orzo cooking.

- You must serve the orzo right after it's cooked or it will lose its loose, creamy consistency. Five minutes is the most it should stand before serving.

OPTIONS

- For a fully vegetarian dish, use water or vegetable stock in place of chicken stock.

- I also love adding cooked, steamed rapini at the end of cooking.

Pasta with Grilled Leeks, Onions, and Mushrooms

Serves 4 to 6

This recipe was developed for a dinner party for one of my favourite clients. The guests really enjoyed the combination of grilled leeks, tomatoes, and cream, so now it's in the book for you to try. Keep in mind that the sauce is a little rich, but you can eliminate the cream or decrease it. If you ever catch a glimpse of baby leeks available in the spring, they are perfect in this recipe. If not, regular leeks will suffice.

1	Portobello mushroom, stem removed	*1*
1	small Vidalia onion, quartered	*1*
6-8	baby leeks (or the whites of 3 large leeks)	*6-8*
3 tbsp	olive oil	*45 mL*
1	bunch fresh basil, chopped	*1*
2	cloves garlic, chopped	*2*
1/2 cup	dry white wine	*125 mL*
2	sprigs fresh thyme, chopped	*2*
3	fresh plum tomatoes, seeded and chopped	*3*
1/2 cup	35% cream	*125 mL*
	Salt and pepper, to taste	
1 lb	pasta	*454 g*
	Fresh Parmesan cheese (optional)	

PREP

- When a barbecue is available, I would grill all the vegetables first and then start putting together the sauce.
- Once the sauce is simmering away with the grilled vegetables, you can start cooking your pasta to time everything properly.

OPTION

- Feel free to add just a touch of the cream to round out the sauce. I would then reduce the white wine to 50 mL (1/4 cup) or the sauce will have too much acidity.

Combine mushroom, onion, and leeks in 30 mL (2 tbsp) olive oil and add basil. Toss in a bowl. Grill. Chop vegetables in smaller pieces and set aside.

In medium saucepan, sauté garlic in the remaining olive oil until soft. Add wine, thyme, and tomatoes and simmer until slightly thickened. Add cream and grilled vegetables and simmer until thickened, about 5 minutes. Season with salt and pepper.

Cook pasta in rolling, boiling, salted water until tender. Drain and toss with sauce. Sprinkle with Parmesan cheese, if desired.

Sautéed Shrimp over Penne in Tomato Fennel Sauce

Serves 4

Shrimp is a great addition to pasta, and in this recipe the flavours are in true harmony. The fennel adds a touch of anise, while the tomatoes are a quick way to keep things zesty. The whole dish takes about 30 minutes to prepare from raw ingredients to table.

1 tbsp	olive oil	15 mL
2	large cloves garlic, finely chopped	2
1	large shallot, finely chopped	1
1/8 tsp	saffron	0.5 mL
12	large shrimp, peeled and deveined	12
1/3 cup	dry vermouth or white wine	75 mL
2 cups	penne	500 mL
4	plum tomatoes (canned), chopped	4
1/2 cup	chopped fennel	125 mL
2 tbsp	sour cream	30 mL
	Salt and freshly ground black pepper, to taste	
2 tbsp	chopped fresh parsley	30 mL

Heat oil on high in medium skillet. When oil is very hot, add garlic, shallot, and saffron. Stirring continuously, sauté for 2 minutes. Immediately add shrimp and toss rapidly for 2 minutes. Shrimp should be just pink and still opaque. Remove pan from heat and add vermouth. Remove shrimp only from pan and set aside.

Meanwhile, cook pasta in plenty of boiling water, salted to taste. Do not cook beyond 12 minutes.

Return vermouth to heat and lower heat to medium. Add tomatoes and fennel, cover, and simmer for 8 minutes. Uncover, add sour cream, and simmer for 5 minutes. Add cooked shrimp, season with salt and pepper, bring mixture back to a boil, and remove from heat. Do not overcook.

Drain pasta but do not rinse. Toss with sauce, add parsley, and stir.

PREP

- All ingredients can be chopped the day before and set in the refrigerator. The whole dish takes about 15 minutes to cook.

- Make sure you remove the shrimp very quickly before cooking the sauce. The shrimp are added back for a very short time at the end just to heat them through. Shrimp should be tender, not rubbery.

OPTION

- Try swordfish in place of the shrimp for something different.

Soba Noodle and Vegetable Sauté

Serves 6 to 8

Soba is another word for buckwheat noodles. We're always looking for better ways to keep healthy and fit and still enjoy our food. This recipe fits both those goals. It's great for those who want to eat vegetables but not feel they are missing out on flavour. If you serve this dish with a piece of grilled fish or chicken, you have a perfectly balanced meal.

PREP

- Soba noodles will not hold up as well as semolina (wheat flour) noodles, so it's best to toss them immediately in soy sauce and some vegetable oil to keep them from sticking. They will taste fine even at room temperature.

- Once the noodles are cooked, it's just a matter of stir-frying your favourite veggies in the spices and ginger and, presto, you've got a delicious dish.

OPTIONS

- This dish can be served as a salad. The longer it sits, the more intense the flavours will be. It contains no animal fat, other than what you serve on the side, so the noodles taste great at room temperature.

- Snow peas can be used instead of snap peas.

7 oz	soba noodles (buckwheat)	*199 g*
1 tbsp	vegetable oil	*15 mL*
2 tbsp	good-quality soy sauce	*30 mL*
1/2 tsp	chile oil	*2 mL*
1 tsp	toasted sesame oil	*5 mL*
1 tbsp	grated fresh ginger	*15 mL*
1	large onion, sliced	*1*
1	large clove garlic, finely chopped	*1*
	Zest of 1 lime, finely grated	
1-1/2 cups	sugar snap peas, blanched	*375 mL*
1	yellow pepper, julienned	*1*
2 tsp	black sesame seeds	*10 mL*
1 tbsp	each rice wine vinegar and lime juice	*15 mL*
1/3 cup	toasted, salted peanuts	*75 mL*
3	green onions, sliced	*3*

Boil soba noodles in rapidly boiling salted water for 4 to 5 minutes, or until just tender. Drain immediately and rinse in cold water. Toss in bowl with vegetable oil and 15 mL (1 tbsp) soy sauce.

Meanwhile, in large skillet, heat chile oil and sesame oil. Add ginger, onion, garlic, and lime zest, and sauté on high for 2 minutes, or until golden. Add snap peas, yellow pepper, and sesame seeds and toss for a few minutes. Add remaining soy sauce and remove from heat.

Add vinegar and lime juice to noodles and toss well. Combine noodles with warm vegetables. Add toasted peanuts and green onions. Toss well. Can be served at room temperature with your favourite grilled fish or chicken.

Spätzle

Serves 4

I just had to include this homemade pasta recipe. It's a staple in Germany and much easier to make than traditional Italian pasta. We made it quite frequently at a health spa that I worked at about 10 years ago. It's quite addictive, so try not to make too much at a time. It's a perfect side dish to any pork, veal, or even a roast chicken dish. For best results, read my notes in Prep.

1 lb	all-purpose flour (about 3-1/2 cups/875 mL)	*454 g*
Pinch	salt	*Pinch*
2	eggs, beaten	*2*
1-1/2-1-3/4 cups	water (enough to achieve a loose batter)	*375-425 mL*

Herb butter

1/4 cup	butter	*50 mL*
1 tsp	chopped fresh rosemary	*5 mL*
	Freshly cracked black pepper, to taste	

In large, deep stockpot, bring to a boil at least 2.5 L (10 cups) of water, salted generously.

Meanwhile, sift flour with salt in a large bowl. Make a well in the centre. Combine eggs with 3/4 of water in small bowl until blended. Slowly pour egg mixture into well. Stir with wooden spoon, gradually taking in more and more of the flour mixture as you turn. Then slowly pour in remaining water only until a smooth but thick batter is achieved.

Meanwhile, melt butter until almost golden and add rosemary and pepper. Keep gently warming on back burner while spätzle is cooking.

Pour about 175 mL (3/4 cup) of batter through a colander or spätzle press over the rolling, boiling water and use a spatula or pastry scraper to press batter through. Cook for 2 to 3 minutes, or until tender. Using a large slotted spoon, remove cooked spätzle to bowl, drizzle with some herb butter and toss. Repeat with remaining batter.

PREP

- Use a wooden spoon and make a well in the centre of dry ingredients before beginning to stir. Stirring gently, gradually take in a little more of the flour. Do not whisk or stir vigorously, or you will get glue. When the batter is ready, it will be fairly loose—a little thicker than pancake batter.

- The ideal way to make the spätzle is in a press, but I always make it over a colander that sits right on top of the pot with boiling water. The holes in the colander should be about about 3 mm (1/8 in) round or spätzle will be too skinny.

- The spätzle cooks very quickly, so prepare the herb butter before cooking. As you scoop out the cooked spätzle, toss it with butter immediately.

OPTION

- Serve this as a side dish instead of potatoes or rice. It's not meant to be the main dish.

Spaghetti al Vongole

Serves 4 to 6

Spaghetti with clam sauce has been made for ages in Italy. The blend of tangy lemon and white wine, spicy chile, and tender pasta clams, and the blast of freshly chopped parsley leave everyone asking for more. Any time you're trying a recipe such as this, it's critical to use the very best ingredients, from the olive oil to the clams. And don't underestimate the power of fresh parsley; wait till you taste what it does here.

1/4 cup	extra virgin olive oil	*50 mL*
4-5	cloves garlic, peeled and finely sliced	*4-5*
1/4 tsp	finely minced chile (or dried flakes)	*1 mL*
1 tbsp	capers	*15 mL*
1 cup	dry white wine	*250 mL*
1/2 cup	fish stock or clam juice	*125 mL*
	Grated zest of 1 lemon	
	Juice of 1/2 lemon	
	Salt and freshly cracked black pepper, to taste	
2-1/2 lb	clams (preferably small pasta variety), well scrubbed and washed	*1.14 kg*
1/2 cup	chopped fresh parsley	*125 mL*
1/4 cup	chopped fresh chives	*50 mL*
1 lb	good-quality spaghetti	*454 g*

In large, deep sauté pan or skillet, heat olive oil on medium. Add garlic and chile and cook over medium heat, stirring frequently until garlic starts to turn golden (it will become bitter if cooked beyond this stage). Remove from heat and add capers, wine, fish stock, lemon zest, lemon juice, and pepper, and return to heat. Add clams, cover, and cook over medium heat until clams open, about 8 to 10 minutes. Remove clams with slotted spoon and reserve until pasta is cooked. Continue to cook sauce until reduced by 1/3. Add parsley and chives.

Meanwhile, bring large pot of salted water to boil over high heat. Cook spaghetti until al dente, about 7 to 8 minutes. Drain and toss immediately into sauce. Add clams and toss for 2 minutes until pasta absorbs some of the sauce. Adjust seasoning and serve immediately.

Note: If sauce has cooled by the time pasta is cooked, simply bring to a boil before tossing in pasta.

PREP

- Once you've cooked the clams, you can put on the pasta. Or you can remove the clams, reduce the sauce, and set everything aside until you're ready to cook the pasta.
- Be sure to wash the clams thoroughly, as they trap a lot of dirt.
- I leave the shells on the clams to reduce preparation time. It also makes for better presentation.
- Don't use dried parsley instead of fresh—it provides way too much flavour.
- If you're not sure what kind of clams to buy, ask your fishmonger.

OPTIONS

- You can add mussels or other seafood to the sauce; simply remove them with the clams.
- If you don't have fish stock, use clam juice.

Wild Mushroom and Herb Pasta

If you're tired of light pasta dishes being tasteless, have I got a recipe for you! Using stock and reducing it with wine, herbs, and onions is a great way to get maximum flavour without all the fat. Besides, it's a break from the typical tomato-based sauces.

Serves 4 to 6

3 cups	veal or chicken stock	*750 mL*
1/2 cup	chopped shiitake mushrooms	*125 mL*
3	cloves garlic, 1 crushed, 2 chopped	*3*
	Freshly cracked black pepper, to taste	
1	sprig each of thyme, rosemary, tarragon, and oregano	*1*
1-1/2 tbsp	olive oil	*22 mL*
1/2	medium onion, chopped	*1/2*
3-4	large oyster mushrooms, gently torn by hand	*3-4*
2 tbsp	madeira	*30 mL*
1 lb	pasta of your choice	*454 g*
2 tbsp	chopped fresh herbs	*30 mL*
	Parmesan cheese, freshly grated	

In medium saucepan, combine stock, shiitake mushrooms, crushed garlic, pepper, and sprigs of herbs. Simmer over medium heat until reduced by 1/2.

In medium frying pan, heat olive oil over high heat, add chopped garlic and onion, and sauté gently until lightly browned. Add oyster mushrooms and continue to cook for a few minutes. Lower heat and add reduced stock and madeira and stir. Remove from heat.

In separate pot, cook pasta in boiling, salted water for 7 to 10 minutes. Drain and add to reduced stock. Add chopped herbs and return to heat. Tosss well until heated through and serve with Parmesan cheese.

PREP
- The method is very similar to other recipes in the book that require you to reduce a sauce, then cook your pasta and combine the two at the end.

OPTION
- For a vegetarian dish, simply use vegetable stock instead of meat or chicken.

Rosemary, Thyme, and Shallot Flat Bread

Serves 8

Bread is generally a labour-intensive endeavour, but this recipe is fairly simple. I don't know about you, but I love flat bread. This one has all kinds of herbs and shallots sautéed and sprinkled on top to make a great crust. Plus, think of all the frustration you can eliminate by kneading some dough in your very own hands!

1 tsp	sugar	*5 mL*
10-12 oz	lukewarm water	*284-340 mL*
1	package dry yeast	*1*
3/4 cup	wheat flour bread flour	*175 mL*
2-1/4 cups	unbleached white flour bread flour	*550 mL*
1-1/2 tsp	salt	*7 mL*
1/4 cup + 1 tbsp	olive oil	*65 mL*
2	fresh shallots, chopped	*2*
	Freshly cracked black pepper, to taste	
1 tbsp	each chopped fresh rosemary and chopped fresh thyme	*15 mL*
	Freshly grated Parmesan cheese (optional)	

In medium bowl, mix together sugar and water and whisk in yeast. Let stand until slightly foamy, about 5 minutes. In food processor or mixer, combine dry ingredients. Add yeast mixture to dry ingredients and combine. Add 50 mL (1/4 cup) olive oil and begin to work dough. Amount of liquid may need adjusting, depending on humidity and other factors. Turn dough onto well-floured surface and knead until smooth and elastic. If dough seems too sticky, add a little more flour when kneading. Place dough in lightly oiled medium bowl and cover with plastic wrap. Let rise in a warm place (29°C/85°F) until doubled, about 90 minutes. Punch down and let stand again for about 30 minutes.

Preheat oven to 190°C (375°F).

Meanwhile, in medium frying pan, combine 15 mL (1 tbsp) oil, shallots, pepper, and herbs and sauté slightly. Cool.

Line baking pan with parchment or olive oil and roll dough into an oblong shape about 1 cm (1/2 in) thick. Score in diagonal lines with sharp knife. Spread shallot mixture over top and sprinkle with cheese, if desired. Let rise in a warm place for 20 minutes before baking.

Bake in oven for 35 minutes, or until golden.

PREP

- Bread preparation depends on humidity and many other factors. Try to use flour as needed. Don't think that you can't use more than the recipe calls for.

- Ideally, making bread is a weekend project, because it does take time to rise.

- Make sure you check the date on the yeast, and always buy more than one package in case it doesn't work.

- Adding the yeast to the warm water and sugar and letting it foam is your insurance that the yeast is alive. If it doesn't foam, don't add it to the recipe.

OPTION

- If you're in a hurry, you can buy frozen bread dough. Take it out of the freezer in the morning before work. When you get home, all you have to do is make this great topping, roll out the dough, and bake it.

Pita Pizzas

Serves 4

This is the recipe that I made on my audition for *Dish It Out*. Here I am, so it must have made an impact. Actually, my producer loved its simplicity. It's also a great example of a dish that tries to introduce you to different kinds of cheese and toppings in an otherwise common dish. It turns the ordinary into the fabulous effortlessly. I also call this the perfect '90s recipe, because it can be custom-designed for families in which everyone arrives home at all hours of the evening.

4	6-in/15-cm Greek-style pitas (soft)	*4*
3 tbsp	extra virgin olive oil	*45 mL*
4 oz	Friulano cheese, shredded	*114 g*
3 oz	goat cheese, crumbled	*85 g*
1/4 cup	black olives, pitted and sliced	*50 mL*
2	plum tomatoes, diced	*2*
2	baby eggplants, grilled and diced	*2*
3	large sprigs fresh basil	*3*
	Freshly cracked black pepper, to taste	

Preheat oven to 200°C (400°F).

Brush olive oil liberally over pitas.

Sprinkle with 1/2 the Friulano, then goat cheese. Sprinkle with olives, tomatoes, and eggplant. Sprinkle with remaining Friulano and top with basil and pepper.

Bake on bottom rack of oven on a cookie sheet for 8 minutes, or until cheese melts and pita is golden. For a crispier crust, place pitas on foil to bake, instead of on a baking sheet.

Cut each pizza into 4 triangles and serve warm.

PREP

- The pitas you need for best results contain yoghurt or something similar. Look for Greek-style pitas or yoghurt in the ingredients.

- These pitas make a great crust that tastes like homemade.

OPTION

- Use any creamy cheese that you can dream of. I would caution you not to overload the pizza with heavy, wet ingredients.

Pissaladière

Serves 6

This is a very popular pizza served in the south of France. It is unique in that it features no tomato sauce. Instead, you have a delicious sweet onion reduction that provides a great backdrop to the salty anchovies and fresh tomatoes. Variety is the spice of life, so you may want to try this recipe, ideally served as an appetizer.

2 tbsp	extra virgin olive oil	*30 mL*
3	large onions (about 8 cups/2 L), sliced	*3*
1	sprig fresh thyme	*1*
	Salt and freshly ground black pepper, to taste	
1	batch pizza dough (recipe follows or use frozen)	*1*
1	small can (2 oz/57 g) anchovies	*1*
4	medium plum tomatoes, sliced	*4*
12	kalamata olives, pitted and sliced	*12*
1 tbsp	chopped fresh herbs	*15 mL*

OPTIONS

• To reduce the quantity of anchovies, slice them into very thin strips before laying them on onions.

• Traditionally this pizza is made with puff pastry, but I find it too rich that way.

In medium saucepan, combine oil, onions, thyme, salt, and pepper and cook over low heat, stirring frequently, until onions begin to soften and take on a caramel colour, about 30 minutes. Stir to ensure onions don't stick to bottom. Mixture is done when onions are caramelized and liquid has reduced completely.

While onions are cooking, slice remaining ingredients.

Preheat oven to 230°C (450°F).

Roll pizza dough onto oiled baking sheet. Dough should be rolled out thinly to ensure a crispy crust. Arrange cooled onion mixture over entire surface of dough. Arrange anchovies in a diagonal pattern over top of onions, then place tomato slice in each diamond between anchovies and sprinkle with olives. Sprinkle with chopped herbs. Bake on bottom rack of oven until crust is crisp, about 20 minutes.

Pizza Dough

2 tbsp	sugar	*30 mL*
1-1/4-1-1/2 cups	lukewarm water	*300-375 mL*
1	package dry yeast	*1*
3 cups	all-purpose flour	*750 mL*
1-1/2 tsp	salt	*7 mL*
1/4 cup	olive oil	*50 mL*

In medium bowl, mix sugar and water and whisk in yeast. Let stand until slightly foamy, about 5 minutes. In a mixer with dough hook, combine flour and salt.

Add yeast mixture to dry ingredients and combine. Add olive oil and begin to work the dough. Dough should be worked until smooth and not sticky. Amount of liquid may need adjusting. If dough seems too sticky, add a little flour and knead.

Place in lightly oiled medium bowl and cover until doubled (about 90 minutes). Punch down and let stand again for 30 minutes.

PREP

- Dough can be made with a plastic attachment on a food processor instead of the steel blade. Keep adding the liquid and pulse until dough is just coming together. Finish the kneading process on a well-floured surface until dough is smooth and elastic.

- Dough can be frozen at any point: before rising, after rising, or even after rolling.

- You can also use frozen dough, or some Italian grocers sell chilled pizza dough that is quite good.

Sun Up

Buckwheat Pancakes with Caramelized Apples

Makes 16 medium pancakes (serves 6 to 8)

This recipe was one that I developed for some viewers who requested breakfast and brunch ideas. I put my thinking cap on and tried to come up with some interesting ways to jazz up breakfast—which happens to be my favourite meal. These pancakes have fibre and a delicious nutty taste because of the buckwheat flour. The caramelized apples further accent that nutty amber taste.

PREP

- Use eggs and milk at room temperature to ensure proper blending of the melted butter.
- Stir the wet ingredients into dry using the well technique only until moistened. Do not whisk or continue to beat, or gluten in flour will develop and create a tough pancake. Ideally you should have some small lumps in batter when you let it rest.
- Always cook pancakes just before serving.

3/4 cup	all-purpose flour	*175 mL*
1/2 cup	buckwheat flour	*125 mL*
2 tsp	baking powder	*10 mL*
Pinch	salt	*Pinch*
2	eggs, room temperature	*2*
1 cup + 2 tbsp	milk, room temperature	*280 mL*
1 tbsp	buckwheat honey (or any other type)	*15 mL*
2 tbsp	melted butter	*30 mL*
	Melted butter (for cooking pancakes)	

Apples

1 tsp	butter	*15 mL*
2 tbsp	sugar	*30 mL*
1	large Matsu or other firm cooking apple, peeled, cored, and thinly sliced	*1*
1/2 tsp	chopped fresh ginger	*2 mL*
1/4 tsp	cinnamon	*1 mL*
1/3 cup	maple syrup	*75 mL*

In medium bowl, sift together flours, baking powder, and salt.

In another medium bowl, whisk together eggs, milk, honey, and butter. Make a well in the centre of dry ingredients and gradually stir in wet ingredients until just combined. Cover and let rest in fridge for at least 30 minutes. Stir again before cooking, just to break any lumps.

Just before making pancakes, prepare apples by heating butter and sugar in medium skillet on high. When sugar is beginning to turn amber, add apple and ginger and toss for 3 to 5 minutes, or until apples are just beginning to soften and are well coated in sauce. Add cinnamon and maple syrup and remove from heat.

Cook pancakes on griddle or shallow skillet, using 5 mL (1 tsp) melted butter at a time. Heat pan or griddle well and pour 50 mL (1/4 cup) batter at a time and cook until pancake begins to bubble on surface. Flip and continue to cook for 1 minute, or until golden. Repeat with remaining batter. Serve with warmed apple mixture.

OPTIONS

- It's hard to substitute other types of flour because this recipe is perfectly balanced with the buckwheat and all-purpose flours. Buckwheat flour is easy to find in health stores and some gourmet shops.

- If you want pancakes that are even fluffier, separate the yolks from the whites and whip the whites separately.

Corn Dill Muffins

Makes 12 large muffins

These savoury muffins are great for breakfast, lunch, or even dinner as an alternative to bread. For brunch, I would serve them with fresh cream cheese and some thinly sliced smoked salmon.

1-1/2 cup	all-purpose flour, sifted	*375 mL*
1/2 cup	cornmeal	*125 mL*
1/2 tsp	salt	*2 mL*
2 tbsp	sugar	*30 mL*
1 tsp	baking powder	*5 mL*
1/2 tsp	baking soda	*2 mL*
1/2 tsp	freshly cracked black pepper	*2 mL*
1	egg	*1*
1	egg white	*1*
3/4 cup	buttermilk	*175 mL*
1/3 cup	vegetable oil	*75 mL*
2 tsp	chopped fresh dill	*30 mL*

Preheat oven to 180°C (350°F).

Brush muffin tins with oil. Set aside.

Combine all dry ingredients, except dill, and stir until well combined. In another bowl, combine egg, egg white, buttermilk, and vegetable oil and whisk until combined. Add dill.

Pour wet ingredients into dry ingredients and stir gently with wooden spoon or rubber spatula until just combined and some flour still appears. Do not mix until smooth or muffins will be tough.

Pour batter into muffin tins and bake for 15 to 20 minutes, or until golden and tester comes out dry from centre of muffin. Remove muffins from tins and cool on wire rack.

PREP

- One simple rule of thumb applies to all muffins: Do not overmix!

OPTIONS

- For the perfect brunch fare, serve with cream cheese, capers, thinly sliced red onions, and smoked salmon.

- Use mini muffin tins and bake about 30 of these as appetizers. I like to top them with slices of smoked trout or combine the smoked trout with cream cheese and make a mousse. They're yummy.

Pear and Cranberry Muffins

I developed this recipe for my clients at Canada Life Assurance Company. I did a bunch of low-fat cooking demos for them and this was one of their favourite recipes. This recipe is not strictly low fat, but it doesn't contain all the fat and sugar that most muffins do. And since I have yet to taste a commercially made low-fat muffin that is not gummy and tasteless, I thought you should be able to make one. Here it is.

**Makes 12
medium muffins**

1-2/3 cups	all-purpose flour, sifted	*400 mL*
1/2 cup	bran	*125 mL*
1/2 tsp	cinnamon	*2 mL*
Pinch	cloves, ground	*Pinch*
1/2 tsp	baking soda	*2 mL*
1 tsp	baking powder	*5 mL*
Pinch	salt	*Pinch*
1/2 cup	each sugar and dried cranberries	*125 mL*
1/2 cup	pear juice	*125 mL*
1	egg	*1*
1/4 cup	vegetable oil	*50 mL*
1/2 cup	buttermilk	*125 mL*
1 tsp	vanilla	*5 mL*

Preheat oven to 180°C (350°F).

Prepare medium muffin tins by brushing or spraying with oil or lining with papers.

In medium bowl, sift together all dry ingredients, except sugar and cranberries. Add sugar and cranberries and stir to combine.

In medium bowl, combine wet ingredients and whisk until combined. Pour wet ingredients into dry ingredients and stir with wooden spoon until just combined and some flour still remains visible. Do not overmix.

Spoon batter into muffin tins. Bake on middle rack of oven for 25 minutes, or until golden.

PREP

- Follow directions for the perfect muffin in the recipe for Corn Dill Muffins on page 170.

OPTION

- You should never change the proportions and ingredients of tested pastry recipes, because they are balanced. You can, however, change the dried cranberries to dried blueberries, currants, sour cherries, etc.

Buttermilk Semolina Biscuits

Makes 8 to 10 biscuits

PREP

- Semolina is a fine, granular, yellow wheat that can be found in most Italian markets.

- The secret to making perfect biscuits is using very cold butter. After adding the liquid, gather the dough until it holds together, as opposed to working it with your hands, which melts the butter and creates tough dough.

- You can cut out the biscuits, place them on baking sheets, and put them in the freezer. In the morning, preheat your oven and bake the dough.

OPTION

- Slice the cooked biscuits in half to create your own mini sandwiches. I use pancetta (Italian bacon), scrambled eggs, a thin slice of smoked mozzarella, and a slice of tomato. These are ideal for guests, because you can let them assemble their own.

These are light, crispy biscuits that you can serve on their own with preserves. Or, you can make what I call the Italian egg muffaletta—my version of an egg muffin with a ton more flavour. If you serve these at brunch, make huge quantities because people will be asking for seconds.

1-1/2 cups	all-purpose flour	*375 mL*
1/3 cup	fine semolina	*75 mL*
1-1/2 tsp	baking powder	*7 mL*
1 tsp	baking soda	*5 mL*
1/2 tsp	salt	*2 mL*
1/3 cup	very cold butter, cut into small pieces	*75 mL*
2/3 cup	buttermilk	*150 mL*
2 tbsp	honey	*30 mL*
1	egg	*1*
1 tbsp	water	*15 mL*

Preheat oven to 190°C (375°F).

In medium bowl, combine flour, semolina, baking powder, baking soda, and salt. Stir until blended. Transfer to food processor fitted with a blade. Add butter and pulse several times until mixture resembles coarse meal.

Meanwhile, whisk together buttermilk and honey. Add buttermilk mixture to flour mixture all at once. Pulse several times, just until mixture starts to come together. Turn onto lightly floured surface and gather dough together. Do not touch too much! Wrap in parchment or waxed paper and chill for 30 minutes.

Roll dough on lightly floured surface to thickness of 1 cm (1/2 in). Using a 6-cm (2-1/2-in) cookie cutter round, cut 8 to 10 rounds and place on baking sheet lined with parchment paper.

Mix egg and water. Brush biscuits with egg mixture and bake until golden and lightly browned on bottom, about 12 to 15 minutes. Cool and slice. Serve with favourite accompaniments.

A Little Something Sweet

Hazelnut Caramel Profiteroles

Makes 20 profiteroles

Profiteroles are cream puffs in disguise. As with any kind of pastry, they require some practice. Don't get frustrated, but try to follow the directions precisely, especially when it comes to measuring the ingredients. Baking requires a different kind of precision, so forget all my speeches about not measuring ingredients. Choux pastry is so versatile that you can fill it with almost anything. In this recipe I toasted some hazelnuts and folded them right into the cream. Plus, you have a creamy caramel and a bittersweet chocolate sauce to play with.

Choux pastry

1/2 cup	all-purpose flour	*125 mL*
1/2 tsp	salt	*2 mL*
1/2 cup	water	*125 mL*
1/4 cup	butter, cut into small pieces	*50 mL*
2	large eggs	*2*

Preheat oven to 190°C (375°F).

Sift flour with salt and set aside. In heavy saucepan, heat water over medium heat and add butter until mixture comes to a boil. Immediately add flour mixture all at once and stir with wooden spoon. Remove mixture from heat and continue beating until it comes away from the side of the pan. Return to heat and stir slightly longer to dry mixture. Remove mixture from heat and add eggs, one at a time, while beating with the wooden spoon until mixture is shiny and falls from the spoon. Fill medium piping bag fitted with medium plain tip and pipe rounds onto baking sheets covered with parchment. Be sure to leave at least 2.5 cm (1 in) between rounds. Bake until brown and hollow sounding, about 20 minutes.

Cream filling

1 cup	35% cream, cold	*250 mL*
2 tbsp	icing sugar	*30 mL*
1/2 cup	chopped toasted hazelnuts	*125 mL*
1/2 tsp	vanilla extract	*2 mL*

PREP

- Choux pastry requires a dry oven, so if you have a convection setting on your oven this is perfect time to use it.

- Try to avoid opening the oven door until the pastry has puffed and is almost cooked. Once they look golden, it is safe to open the door. Pick one up and tap the bottom to see if it sounds hollow.

- Once piped and baked, choux can be cooled and frozen in well-sealed bags. Once thawed, it can be dried in the oven for 2 to 4 minutes, just until crisp.

- Chocolate and caramel sauces can be made in advance and kept at room temperature until ready to serve, or kept in the fridge for several days and warmed just before serving to soften.

In cold stainless steel bowl, whip cream until peaks begin to form. Add icing sugar and continue to beat for 30 seconds, until soft peaks hold. Fold in nuts and stir in vanilla. Cover with plastic wrap and store in fridge until ready to assemble puffs.

Caramel sauce

1/2 cup	sugar	*125 mL*
1/3 cup	35% cream	*75 mL*
1 tbsp	dark rum	*15 mL*

In heavy-bottom pot, cook sugar on high until it begins to smoke and turns amber. Remove from heat immediately and add cream. Let stand for several minutes until mixture stops bubbling. Add rum and cook for 1 minute if you want to boil off alcohol. Stir well until smooth. Cool.

Chocolate sauce

1/2 cup	milk or cream	*125 mL*
4 oz	bittersweet chocolate, chopped	*114 g*
1 tbsp	brandy (optional)	*15 mL*

In medium pot, bring milk to a boil and pour over chocolate. Let stand until chocolate melts and stir with a wooden spoon. Add brandy and stir well.

To assemble, cut cream puffs in half, horizontally. Pipe a large rosette of whipped cream and cover with the top of puff. Drizzle with chocolate sauce. Lay on a plate and drizzle with caramel sauce.

OPTIONS

- Add slices of banana on the bottom layer of the puff before piping cream on top.
- For a quicker recipe, leave out the sauces and simply dust the filled puffs with icing sugar and cocoa just before serving.

No-Fat Fruit Terrine

Serves 6 to 8

There are few desserts that are low in fat but taste delicious. This is a recipe I developed recently for a low-fat cooking class. It's basically a homemade Jell-O that uses all-natural ingredients such as puréed pears, orange juice, and fresh berries. Once you add the late harvest wine, the flavour just jumps out at you. If you make this without the crème anglaise, it's completely fat free! Because you make it in a loaf pan and slice it, the result is a sophisticated, colourful, easy-to-make dessert.

1/2 cup	orange juice	*125 mL*
	Juice of 1/2 lemon	
1	package (1 tbsp/15 mL) plain gelatin	*1*
3	medium pear halves, puréed, canned or fresh	*3*
1/2 cup	sugar	*125 mL*
1/4 cup	sauternes or any late harvest wine	*50 mL*
3 cups	assorted fresh fruit and berries	*750 mL*

Combine orange juice and lemon juice in small bowl. Sprinkle gelatin over top and let stand for 2 minutes, until gelatin softens.

In small saucepan, combine pear, sugar, and sauternes. Bring to a boil. Remove from heat, stirring until sugar dissolves. While mixture is still hot, add gelatin mixture. Stir until well dissolved.

Pour about 50 mL (1/4 cup) pear mixture into the bottom of a small loaf pan and place in fridge until set, about 20 minutes. Cover with a layer of assorted fruit, then with more pear mixture. Set again until firm, about 40 minutes. Repeat until all fruit is used, ending with pear mixture.

PREP

- If you are in a hurry, you can simply pour all of the pear mixture into the loaf pan and add the fruit. You will not get the layered effect, but all the taste will still be there.

OPTION

- To make this terrine for kids, substitute orange juice for the wine.

Light Crème Anglaise

2	egg yolks	2
2 tbsp	sugar	30 mL
1 cup	1% milk, cold	250 mL
2 tbsp	cornstarch	30 mL
1/2 tsp	vanilla	2 mL

Place egg yolks in small bowl and add sugar. Whisk several minutes until smooth and pale. In small saucepan, combine milk and cornstarch. Whisk until cornstarch dissolves. Stir over medium heat until boiling and thickened, about 3 to 5 minutes.

Pour hot milk mixture slowly into egg mixture, whisking quickly. Return to medium heat, stirring with wooden spoon. Continue to heat just until mixture comes to a boil, but do not boil rapidly. Remove from heat and let cool completely, stirring occasionally. Add vanilla and stir.

To serve, immerse bottom of loaf pan in warm water for 30 seconds and it will start to melt. Flip terrine over, slice, and serve with sauce.

Kir-Poached Pears
with Vanilla Crème Anglaise

Serves 4 to 6

PREP

- When selecting pears for poaching, make sure they are ripe but still firm. If you use very hard pears, the poaching liquid will not penetrate and the texture will be rough.

- Placing parchment paper right on the surface of the pears ensures that they are immersed and evenly poaching.

- A proper crème anglaise should never be boiled. It takes a little practice, but try to remove the custard from the heat before it has completely thickened, as it will continue to cook. The best way to check it is to run your finger across the back of the spoon; if the mark of your finger stays, it is ready.

OPTIONS

- For a lighter crème anglaise, see the recipe with No-Fat Fruit Terrine (page 176).

- This dish also can be served with vanilla ice cream.

Poached pears are a fabulous fall and winter dessert when the fruit is in its prime. Remember: Simplicity can be very impressive if executed properly. This dessert also keeps well in the fridge and can be pulled out for those unexpected guests. If I feel like having something a little sweet but not heavy, this is the one I go for.

4 cups	water	*1 L*
1 cup	sugar	*250 mL*
4	bosc or other pears, ripe but firm	*4*
	Juice of 1/2 lemon	
1 cup	kir, brandy, or sweet red wine	*250 mL*
2	strips lemon zest, peeled with knife	*2*
1	cinnamon stick	*1*
2	whole cloves	*2*

In large pot, bring water and sugar to a boil. Meanwhile, peel pears and cut in half, lengthwise. Immerse in liquid and add juice, kir, lemon zest, cinnamon stick, and cloves. Cover surface of pears with parchment paper. Continue to simmer pears on low heat until very tender, about 40 minutes. Serve with crème anglaise.

Crème Anglaise

2 cups	whole milk	*500 mL*
1/2 cup	sugar	*125 mL*
1/2	vanilla bean, cut in half lengthwise and scraped (or 1/2 tsp/2 mL vanilla extract)	*1/2*
5	egg yolks	*5*

In medium, heavy-bottom pot, combine milk, sugar, and vanilla. Bring just to a boil and remove from heat. Meanwhile, mix egg yolks in small bowl with wooden spoon. Pour a little of the hot milk over yolks while stirring rapidly, just to temper the mixture. Immediately pour this mixture over milk while continuing to mix. Return to medium heat and continue stirring. Mixture is ready when it coats the back of the spoon but has not boiled.

Immediately remove from heat and strain through a fine strainer to remove any egg bits. Put in cold water bath and stir frequently to prevent yolks from cooking.

Coconut Ginger Crème Brûlée

The popularity of crème brûlée has skyrocketed in the last few years. Since it is a fairly simple dessert to make it's included in the *Dish It Out* repertoire, but you know me better than to think I wouldn't give it a twist. This variation has a delicious Caribbean theme, with the coconut milk and ginger. It's the perfect dessert for a dinner party because it can be made in advance and you can burn the tops just before serving.

2 cups	35% cream	*500 mL*
3/4 cup	coconut milk	*175 mL*
1/2 cup	milk	*125 mL*
1	vanilla bean, split in half	*1*
1 tbsp	grated fresh ginger, plus 2 thin slices	*15 mL*
1/2 cup	sugar, plus 1/3 cup/75 mL for topping	*125 mL*
8	egg yolks	*8*

Preheat oven to 150°C (300°F).

Heat cream with coconut milk, milk, vanilla bean (scrape out seeds and add to cream), ginger slices, and 1/2 cup of sugar and bring to a boil.

Meanwhile, with a rubber spatula stir together egg yolks in medium bowl. Have a strainer ready over another bowl. When cream comes to a boil, pour slowly over egg yolks while stirring constantly with spatula. Do not whisk. Strain immediately. Skim off any foam, add grated ginger, and stir.

Place ramekins in water bath with water about halfway up the sides of ramekins. Divide custard between ramekins and cover with foil. Transfer carefully and bake on middle rack of oven for 50 to 60 minutes, or until slightly soft in centre when shaken. Remove from bath and let cool to room temperature, about 20 minutes. Cover with plastic wrap, not touching surface. Chill.

Before serving, cook remaining sugar in heavy-bottom pot until it becomes dark amber, about 3 to 4 minutes. Quickly pour 1 heaping spoonful of hot sugar over each custard, working quickly, as sugar is still cooking. Alternately, spoon 30 mL (2 tbsp) sugar on each custard and use a torch to burn sugar.

Yields 8

PREP

- Straining the custard is very important to remove any traces of cooked egg.

- The propane in a torch is highly flammable. The safest way to get a crunchy top is to follow my directions.

- The custards can be made up to 2 days in advance; simply ensure that you leave them at room temperature for about 15 minutes before caramelizing them.

- Never use a convection setting to cook custard.

OPTIONS

- For a classical brûlée, replace the milk and coconut milk with the same amount of cream and leave out the ginger.

- It is impossible to make a low-fat crème brûlée. Another option is to make crème caramel, which calls for milk instead of cream and has a slightly rubbery consistency.

Poached Figs in Red Wine and Balsamic Vinegar

Serves 4

This is the simple finale to a late summer or early fall dinner. The key here is to gently poach the figs for a short time, allowing them to keep their shape but infusing them with the rich flavour of the wine and vinegar. If you aren't familiar with or have never tried fresh figs, here's a great opportunity to do so.

1-1/2 cups	fruity red wine	*375 mL*
1/2 cup	balsamic vinegar	*125 mL*
2 tbsp	honey	*30 mL*
1 tbsp	lemon juice	*15 mL*
1	cinnamon stick	*1*
8	medium fresh purple figs	*8*

PREP

- The work here is all in the figs. If you select firm, ripe, delicious figs, the dessert will be divine.
- Do not poach the figs too long or they will lose their delicate flavour.

OPTIONS

- In winter, you can use dried figs and poach them for a little while longer, rehydrating them.
- You can also serve this dessert with vanilla ice cream or gelato.

In medium saucepan, combine wine, vinegar, honey, lemon juice, and cinnamon stick. Bring to a boil and reduce to a simmer. Simmer, uncovered, until reduced by 1/3.

Pierce figs gently with fork to allow poaching liquid to penetrate. Do not peel figs.

Lay figs in poaching liquid and poach over low heat for 10 to 15 minutes, or until figs are plump and still hold their shape. Remove figs from liquid.

Increase heat and boil poaching liquid, uncovered, until reduced and syrupy, about 10 minutes.

Serve figs drizzled with glaze, with a little wafer or biscotti.

Lemon Cornmeal Cookies

These crisp and tangy delights are great all-purpose cookies. They are not too sweet, not too tart, and have just a touch of cornmeal, which gives them a slight crunch. In short, they are just right. They are also not too fussy, because you just drop them onto a baking sheet and press them down with a fork. I'll go put the kettle on.

3/4 cup	soft butter	*175 mL*
1 cup	sugar	*250 mL*
2	eggs	*2*
	Zest of 2 lemons	
1 tbsp	lemon juice	*15 mL*
3/4 tsp	vanilla extract	*3 mL*
1/2 cup	pastry flour	*125 mL*
1/2 cup	all-purpose flour	*125 mL*
1/4 cup	cornmeal	*50 mL*
3/4 tsp	baking powder	*3 mL*
1/8 tsp	baking soda	*0.5 mL*
Pinch	salt	*Pinch*

Preheat over to 180°C (350°F).

Cream butter in medium bowl until fluffy, about 2 minutes. Gradually add sugar, beating well at medium speed. Add eggs, lemon zest, lemon juice, and vanilla and mix well, scraping down sides of bowl.

Combine flours, cornmeal, baking powder, baking soda, and salt and add to creamed mixture. Beat at low speed for 30 seconds, just to combine.

Drop dough onto baking sheet covered with parchment paper, leaving 5 cm (2 in) between cookies. Flatten cookies with fork and bake for 10 to 12 minutes, or until golden. Remove from baking sheet and cool on wire racks.

Yields 3 dozen medium cookies

PREP

- The secret to great cookies is to cream the soft butter before adding the sugar. Once you add the sugar, continue to beat until the mixture is very fluffy. Once you have added the flour, do not keep beating because that creates a tough cookie.

- Try making the cookie dough, dropping it onto the baking sheet, and freezing the whole thing. You can bake it at any time and, presto, you'll have fresh cookies.

OPTIONS

- Substitute semolina for the cornmeal.

- For interesting colour, try using blue fine cornmeal instead of yellow.

- If you're not using parchment paper, you don't need to grease your cookie sheet if it's non-stick.

Oatmeal Oat Bran Cookies

Yields 28 cookies

Here's a great recipe for oatmeal cookies that are chewy and fluffy instead of thin and crispy. They are very fragrant because of the addition of cinnamon, ginger, and apple butter. They make a great snack for the whole family because they are not loaded with fat or too much sugar.

1/2 cup	softened butter	*125 mL*
1/2 cup	brown sugar	*125 mL*
1	egg	*1*
1/4 cup	apple butter	*50 mL*
1 tsp	vanilla	*5 mL*
1 cup	all-purpose flour	*250 mL*
1/2 cup	oat bran	*125 mL*
1/2 cup	quick-cooking oats, uncooked	*125 mL*
1/4 cup	raisins	*50 mL*
1/2 tsp	cinnamon	*2 mL*
1/4 tsp	chopped fresh ginger	*1 mL*
1 tsp	baking powder	*5 mL*
Pinch	salt	*Pinch*
Pinch	nutmeg	*Pinch*

PREP
- Using brown sugar will give you a denser cookie with a little more tang.

OPTIONS
- You can use 0.5 mL (1/8 tsp) ginger powder to replace fresh ginger.
- If you use applesauce instead of apple butter, the cookies will be a little gummy and not as flavourful.

Preheat oven to 180°C (350°F).

In medium bowl, cream butter until fluffy. Add brown sugar and beat at medium speed until light and fluffy, about 5 minutes. Add egg, apple butter, and vanilla and beat well until combined, about 1 minute.

Meanwhile, combine remaining ingredients, add to butter mixture, and beat on low until just combined, about 30 seconds.

Drop dough, 5 mL (1 tsp) at a time, 5 cm (2 in) apart on a baking sheet lined with parchment paper. Bake for 15 minutes, or until golden. Cool.

Index